A More Profound Alleluia!

Gelineau and Routley on Music in Christian Worship

A More Profound Alleluia!

Gelineau and Routley on Music in Christian Worship

Charles S. Pottie, S.J.

The Pastoral Press
Washington, D.C.

ISBN: 0-912405-12-0

© Copyright 1984, The Pastoral Press. All Rights Reserved.

The Pastoral Press
225 Sheridan Street, NW
Washington, D.C. 20011
(202) 723-5800

The Pastoral Press is the publications division of the National Association of Pastoral Musicians, a membership organization of musicians and clergy dedicated to fostering the art of musical liturgy.

Printed in the United States of America

Cover design by Rona Tiffany, Roth Advertising.

Contents

Dedication . . .

To the memory of my mother
and my father,
who taught me how to
"Sing a new song to the Lord,
His praise in the Assembly of the faithful."

Psalm 149

Acknowledgments

My sincere thanks go to all those who have helped in the writing of this book. But special thanks to: Rev. Joseph Mills whose early influence on me in the area of liturgical music was most formative; my superiors whose support and encouragement I continually rely on; my colleagues, the students and staff at Regis College (a member of the Toronto School of Theology) who provide a challenging and supportive atmosphere of theological learning; professors and friends at the Graduate Theological Union in Berkeley; my friends at Boston College; the community at Weston School of Theology for a summer's hospitality to work on this book; to so many others whose lives and friendship reveal for me . . . Christ Jesus, who plays in ten thousand places . . . through the features of human faces (Hopkins).

Introduction

Music and worship are intimately connected; they have been so since their pagan and Judaic origins,[1] since the beginning of Christian worship, and throughout the history of the church up to our present day when, more and more, a musical liturgy is the norm.

Because music has played such a prominent and integral role in the church's worship life throughout its history, can we not discover and articulate some of its theological meaning? Does not the use of music in our common worship say and speak something of the God of Jesus Christ and his kingdom? Does not the kind and placement of music at worship tell us something about God and his covenant with humanity? Can we not articulate theological criteria for music at worship that would help us in the practical task of choosing and actually performing music in our services? Can we leave this important element, this rich symbol of Christian worship and ritual to our whims and fancies, to our tastes and feelings of the moment? Are there not deeper theological principles involved in all the questions of a musical worship or liturgy, of the relationship between music and worship?

It is such a range of questions that led me to explore the writings of these two men, Joseph Gelineau and Erik Routley. I want to present this subject in an ecumenical perspective, taking the writings of two people from different Christian traditions, and offer a summary of what each says about the theological meaning of music in worship. Each of them is a theologian and musician; each has made a notable contribution to a theological understanding of music for worship. Because of their pastoral involvement in the field of music and worship and their theological reflection on it,[2] I have discovered in them two bases, two viewpoints for a furthering of our theological understanding of worship music.

Joseph Gelineau comes out of the Roman Catholic liturgical tradition. Born in 1920, and educated in France, he entered the Society of Jesus in 1941. He studied theology at Lyon-Fourvière and has a diploma in music composition from the Ecole César Franck. He is a doctor of theology and professor of pastoral liturgy and liturgical musicology at the Institut Catholique in Paris. His dissertation thesis was on the forms of psalmody in the Syriac churches of the 4th and 5th centuries. For the past thirty years or so, Gelineau has been closely associated with the Centre de Pastorale Liturgique in Paris. Well known for his melodies of the psalms in the vernacular, he has played a very active role in the present liturgical reforms. He helped found two reviews for liturgical music, *Eglise qui chante* and *Musique et liturgie,* and is also co-founder of *Universa Laus,* an international group for research into the role of singing and music in the liturgy. Besides his numerous musical compositions, Gelineau has written books and numerous articles on music and liturgy. He recently moved from an urban parish in Paris to care for some rural parishes near Paris.

Erik Routley, on the other hand, was a representative of the Reformed, free church worship tradition. He was born in 1917 in Brighton, England. He studied classics and did his theological education as well as his doctor of philosophy degree at Oxford University. His dissertation thesis was on the music of Christian hymnody. He was ordained into the Congregational Church in England and Wales in 1943. After serving as pastor to several congregations in England and Scotland, he became President of the Congregational Church in 1970 and was a leading force in the merger with the Presbyterian Church to form the United Reformed Church of England and Wales in 1972. Routley had a life-long interest in hymnody and church music. From 1948 to 1974, he edited the *Bulletin* of the Hymn Society of Great Britain and Ireland. He edited or composed music for several hymnals and wrote many books and articles on hymnody and church music in Britain and America. He became a Fellow of the Royal School of Church Music in 1965 and a member of the

Council of R.S.C.M. in 1968. Routley moved to the United States in 1975, serving as professor of church music and Director of Chapel at Westminster Choir Chapel in Princeton, New Jersey. He was also associate editor of *Worship* from 1975 until his death in October, 1982.

The purpose of this book is to summarize the main lines and theses of these two men regarding the significance of music for worship. They represent two approaches to the question and provide two pivots and foundations for future theological reflection on music in worship. An added advantage in exploring the writings of these two musician/theologians is the ecumenical perspective. The present century's liturgical renewal, particularly since the Second Vatican Council (1962-1965) has broken through denominational barriers in the Christian community. This has been an enrichment for all the diverse Christian traditions.[3] The liturgical tradition and the place of music within it, represented by Gelineau, and the Reformed, free church tradition and its theological view of music in the worship service, represented by Routley, will give us some contrasts and— surprisingly, perhaps—some similarities in a theological understanding of music in worship. Aided by the reflection of these two Christians, a sense of direction, some underlying criteria and perspectives for the pastoral application of music and worship may emerge.

For both Gelineau and Routley, music in worship has theological meaning because it communicates to the worshiping community the invitation and challenge to fuller life and love with God in Christ.

Each author arrives at this conclusion differently. Gelineau begins with the liturgical assembly and its rites. Routley uses sacred scripture as the foundation for the pattern and shape of God's communication with humankind. For each author, music, when done in the context of the worship action, is not an end in itself. It communicates symbolically the offer and promise of God's life in Christ and our response to this offer and promise. It is interesting that Gelineau emphasizes the role and power of the Word in the unfolding of the liturgical action—and how music completes the spoken word—while Routley ends up emphasizing the dramatic, liturgical element that must be present in every worship service, and how music serves in the unfolding of the drama of worship, even those services where proclaiming and preaching the Word is central. The music of worship has profound theological meaning in both traditions because of its symbolic power to communicate the depth, the height, and the breadth of God's love in Christ to the worshiping community. All art in worship should be a kind of environment, an atmosphere, a symbol to reveal to worshipers God's call and invitation to a fullness of life in Jesus Christ. Music in worship can be nothing less than that.

In a recent address titled "Models Interrelating Art and Worship,"[4] Stephen Happel described five different models that have been operative in one way or another in the church's tradition: worship against art, worship of art, worship above art, worship and art in paradox, and worship as the transformation of art. It is this fifth model that I found most helpful and does, I believe, express the views of both the authors under discussion. Art (in this case, music) works as a partner in the worship activity; worship needs art because we are embodied spirits; art and worship are involved in a mutually beneficial conversation. One frees and enables the other to be what it most deeply is, not without some risk, but to the completion and fullness of both.

PART I:
Joseph Gelineau

Chapter 1:
The Meaning of the Liturgical Assembly in the Church

In celebrating the liturgy is it possible to put across that it is an action in which all take part and that the assembly is the principal "subject"?[1]

Before we can understand why music is of such importance in Christian worship, Gelineau insists that the notion of "l'assemblée liturgique" (the liturgical assembly) must be grasped clearly. We gather together in the name of the Lord and, for that reason, we sing and make music and celebrate with all our human gifts. Gelineau situates the value and meaning of worship music in this context of the liturgical assembly: God's gathered people, here and now, listening and responding to the Word and—if it is Eucharist—giving thanks and sharing in the meal of the Son, and then finally being sent forth to proclaim and live as witnesses of this loving God.

This first chapter will be a summary of Gelineau's understanding of the liturgical assembly in the Christian community. Since celebrating the liturgy is the function of the people assembled and done for the sake of these same gathered people, the assembled people's *self-image* is what is of utmost importance, not simply the right functioning of rites or the relationship of the ministers to the people. This self-image of the worshiping assembly is what enables and contributes to a deep sense of communal celebration.[2] The liturgical assembly contains a profound meaning—a mystery (in Latin, *sacramentum*)—and it functions out of this meaning. The assembly expresses itself in song and music and all forms of art because of the meaning intrinsic to it.

Thus, four aspects of Gelineau's theology of the liturgical assembly will be explored:

1) A sign of the covenant between God and God's people;

2) the characteristics of this assembly;
3) The communication through ritual in this assembly;
4) an assembly to hear God's Word and break bread together.

With this background for understanding the liturgical assembly, music for this assembly's worship will be rooted theologically in the assembled people for worship, rather than in music itself as mere decoration or adjunct to the worship activity.[3]

Sign of the Covenant

Of all the signs that bring about the Covenant, the first one, which is the condition of all the others . . . is the sign of the assembly.[4]

From the beginning of creation, God is revealed to the human family as a God desiring to make a covenant, a bond of mutual love. God has always initiated this love and calls for a free response from human beings. The gift of creation is itself the first sign of a covenant initiated by God. The natural "cult" of a specific group, its worship through prayers, dance, sacrifices, and song, celebrates this creation-covenant. The covenant made with Noah in Genesis (8:20-9:17) is an archetype of all "natural" covenants found and expressed in the cults of different cultures. The created universe is seen, however vaguely, as a covenant sign and is celebrated and remembered by people gathered to acknowledge the provident creator and God of the universe.

Through the history of a specific people—Israel—a new stage of covenant emerges. God is revealed as one who acts in the historical events of this people. God is a redeeming, liberating God in their political and social history. God makes a covenant with this people. And whenever this people assembles, they renew this covenant with their God—as for example, at Sinai (Ex. 19,24,34), at Sichem (Jos. 24), and on the return from the Babylonian exile (Neh. 8,9). In each of these "model" liturgical assemblies, the primary element is the assembly of the people who come together to renew and to reactualize the covenant that God had initiated with them. Gelineau summarizes it in this way:

> The liturgy of Israel . . . re-presents the initiative of God acquiring a people; it recalls the demands of his Law; it renews the "disposition" of the agreement in a ritual sign (sacrifice) which calls for, in its turn, a life conformed to the "justice" of the kingdom of God.[5]

In a final, definitive communication to the human family, God's faithful love is revealed through the humanity of the Son in a new and everlasting covenant through the death and resurrection of that same Jesus. Jesus' work of universal salvation is to assemble all people into the Kingdom of God. After his ascension to the Father and the outpouring of the Spirit at Pentecost, the church—the *ekklesia*—the assembly of those saved in Jesus' name, was born. Since Pentecost, the followers of this Lord Jesus have always somehow gathered together for the purpose of celebrating anew this covenant with God in Jesus Christ. "Hence the liturgy of the New Covenant is: a gathering together, proclamation of the Word, prayer and sacrament, for spiritual worship."[6]

The church is the continuation of the old and yet radically new *"Qahal Yahweh"*—a people gathered in the Name of the Lord to celebrate the new covenant in the death and resurrection of Jesus. This church is most clearly visible as a covenanted people in the local liturgical assemblies where people from diverse backgrounds are gathered in faith, hope, and love to hear God's Word and renew the covenant in some form of ritual activity. Gelineau states clearly that this particular local assembly of the followers of Jesus is not incidental to the liturgical action; instead:

> The gathering together is itself a visible manifestation and historical realization of the gathering of those who are saved. Before every particular liturgical action, word or rite, the assembly is required— "No liturgy without an assembly"—and already the assembly is of itself mystery and sacrament, thanks to the active presence of the Lord.[7]

9

God, in Jesus Christ, has made a final covenant of love with the human family. This is revealed and made visible in the church—the community of believers *throughout* the world. But when a number of these believing people gather in a *specific* place and time in order to renew and actualize once again this new covenant in Christ, then this particular liturgical assembly is a sign of the universal church, which is itself the sacrament of the communion, begun but still to come, of all humanity with God. In Gelineau's view, the liturgical assembly as a sign of the church bears all the marks of our weakness and division, along with the radical unity achieved in Christ. During the liturgical assembly a small number of people from the mass of humanity come together in faith, hope, and love of the covenant in Jesus. The diversity and divisions remain, yet are somehow transcended (feebly it seems at times) in the hope of our full unity and communion in God. The covenant in Jesus is complete, yet still to be realized more fully in us. In the same way, each liturgical assembly shares in the same polarity between what is already and what is not yet. Like the church—on a journey, a pilgrim in this world—:

> . . . the assemblies of the people of God are always partial, local, temporary, imperfect, as we see in the community of Corinth. They are not less the manifestation of the whole body of Christ. They are a "sacrament" of this body.[8]

Thus, the new covenant is experienced and known in faith in the particularity of *each* liturgical assembly. Each liturgical assembly is, in this way, an efficacious sign of the covenant revealed in the whole church.

Some Characteristics of the Liturgical Assembly

Since the liturgical assembly is, in Gelineau's view, a sign, sacrament and symbol that actualizes, here and now, the new covenant in Christ, it is a unique kind of human gathering. But like any human grouping, it has certain tensions and polarities that are characteristic and peculiar to itself. These characteristic polarities within the liturgical assembly must not be suppresed, but recognized and creatively worked through. In the previously cited work, edited by Gelineau, *Dans vos assembleés,* he discusses the following aspects of the liturgical assembly:

a) It is an assembly of those who believe in Christ the Lord that they may thereby grow in deeper faith and lead others to faith in him. Without this basis of faith, the assembly for worship would not have its distinctive meaning. It would simply be another group bound by some common interest or concern. This element of faith, so distinctive of the Christian liturgical assembly, is an obvious tension with both the non-faith or lack of faith in the believers themselves who are gathered for worship, and the unbelief in the world in which they live. The tension cannot be avoided, but must be kept in a creative balance. Faith is the reason for coming together. A deepening and nourishing of faith is the normal result of the gathering for worship. The same faith sends the gathered believers forth into a world hungering for and resisting faith, and urges them to proclaim by their lives the Good News received in faith. As Gelineau states:

> All those who have heard the call of Christ converge at the assembly. And from the assembly leave all those who have received the mission to announce the wonderful deeds of God. Missionary activity which is not incorporated into the church is sterile or misguided. The assembly which does not express its call to mission is dying or lying.[9]

b) The liturgical assembly is both holy and sinful at the same time. Its holiness comes from the fact that it is part of the whole people of God, whom God has called and chosen, redeemed and purified by the blood of the Son to lead lives of holiness according to this call. "The whole liturgy affirms and assumes this holiness of the assembly but especially at the communion of the body and blood of the Lord."[10]

But this gathering is not an elite of "those who are saved"; it consists of those who know and acknowledge their sinful condition before the Holy One. No one in the assembly is fully faithful to God's Word and covenant in Christ. "In every assembly, there are those who are sick, and even those who are 'dead.' "

An authentic assembly of worship is holy but always recognizes its need for reconciliation with the Lord and within itself, because it knows itself as unholy as well.

c) It is an assembly that manifests both a oneness and a disparateness. Its unity comes from the same source as the church's: the power of the Holy Spirit, who enables the members of the assembly to share like thoughts and concerns and to welcome each other in mutual respect and love. Since the universal church

> . . . is open to all those who believe, whatever their race, nationality, class, culture, sex, age, profession, past life, temperament, without discrimination or favoring of persons. . . . [12]

in the same way, the local liturgical assembly must mirror this diversity and richness, even social antimonies, at the same time it recognizes and seeks to witness to the reality of our oneness in Christ, that we are all but one person in Christ Jesus (cf. Gal. 3:28). Each assembly, Gelineau asserts. . . . "must find the way of maintaining its catholicity and of constantly pulling down barriers that it encounters."[13]

d) This assembly is a group of people that is hierarchic in its structure and charismatic in its members. It is hierarchic because Christ is the head of the Body and we are his members, and a similar structure is to be found in the liturgical assembly.[14] The presider of the assembly is like the head of the Body; the members of this Body are constituted by the assembled people. But the assembly is also charismatic—that is, gifted in diverse ways through the Holy Spirit in its individual members. This charismatic character, Gelineau emphasizes, has not always been prominent in the liturgical assembly. But, even though a preference was given to the hierarchic functions in the assembly, the charisms, the gifts of the Spirit, have not been completely absent—such as the gifts of preaching, teaching, and leading song within the assembly. The hierarchic and charismatic elements do not exclude each other. They both come from the same Spirit of

Christ. As far as the exercise of diverse charisms *within* the liturgical assembly and *for* its own well-being, Gelineau sees many possibilities:

> . . . *witnessing to the Word as heard and lived, expressions of prayer, presiding and animating the assembly, creation of hymns and songs. . . . There is also an inexhaustible source of renewal in meaningful forms of art (literary, musical, plastic art forms, celebrational style, etc.)*[15]

Such charisms, when encouraged for the service of the liturgical assembly, renew and add vigor to what can become mere formality or ritualism.

e) The liturgical assembly is a community of unique, individual, free persons. If it were just a collection of individuals, there would not be such a great tension. But in this gathering for worship, the individual person and his or her unique vocation is affirmed at the same time as the life and vocation of the gathered group:

> *Each person must actualize one's deepest personal vocation, at the same time making one's own the ways of the celebrating group. There is a continual tension between the individual who comes to the assembly and the symbolic action which is offered by the liturgy.*[16]

In the liturgical action of the assembly, each person is called to *metanoia*—to conversion—to become a new person in Christ, to freely choose what is celebrated communally by the symbolic actions. The tension is accentuated because sometimes the common ritual actions are not familiar or not understood sufficiently, or they are being done with others whom one does not know well or hardly at all. Hence the individual members seem to be constrained into communal activities where one's personal freedom is not fully respected. But in reality, one needs the other. The community is for the growth and freedom of the individual person, and the person must find himself or herself freely within the community and its symbolic actions in the liturgy. "The Covenant assumes a believing people who are freely involved."[17] The liturgical assembly, being a community of free persons, must live and celebrate that tension creatively.

f) Finally, the liturgical assembly, though primarily cultic (i.e., focusing on prayer and sacraments), needs to be continually related to other forms of Christian assemblies. This is the tension inherent in the assembly gathered for worship because the act of "cultic" worship is not the whole of the Christian life. The act of cultic worship is a central, expressive, and life-giving source for the Christian's life in the world, but where is the teaching function evident as it was in the "teaching of the Apostles" of the primitive Christian communities? Where is the *koinonia*—the fellowship, fraternal love, and common life of Christians—that was practiced in early Christian assemblies? Gelineau seriously questions the one-sidedness of stressing the cultic aspect of our liturgical assembly at the expense of the other functions of Christian assemblies:

> *Where are there "assemblies of the church"—apart from the liturgical—in which questions regarding its life are dealt with? . . . if the liturgical assembly does not identify itself with the local Christian community, this community will need other ways of asserting its existence.*[18]

This tension within the liturgical assembly vis-a-vis other needs of the Christian community, namely, teaching and *koinonia,* can be overlooked only at the risk of being too cultic and losing a sense of the totality of meaning of the Christian assembly.

Each of these characteristics of the liturgical assembly involves a particular tension or polarity. Not only must they be recognized as such, but, when kept in proper balance, they become the means of constant growth and authenticity in the kingdom for the members of each liturgical assembly. As Gelineau expresses it:

> *We have said that the sign value of the assembly (i.e., the group united here and now) was always inadequate to the reality signified (the universal gathering of the people of God). That is the ultimate tension which pastoral liturgy can*

*never cease allowing to appear and which it must make fruit-
ful. . . . Because the sign of the assembly must disappear,
with the sacraments and rites, the ministries and charisms, in
order to let appear the new Jerusalem, where God will be
"with" his people and where the Lamb will be the temple
(Apoc. 21:22).* [19]

The Liturgical Assembly and Communication through Ritual

Christians are first and foremost people who gather
together."[20] But the gathering of Christians for worship
necessarily involves human communication. It is in this liturgical assembly that God communicates with us and we, in
turn, communicate with God and with one another by means
of ritual actions.

The assembly's ritual activity, i.e., the ensemble of signs
and symbols (words, gestures, actions, and objects) has a
definite function. Ritual serves as the medium for the communication in faith between God and us, and we among ourselves, in order to actualize again and again the everlasting
covenant between God and the human family.

Signs and symbols in the liturgical assembly communicate
on two levels: first, they communicate *among* those present
who experience them. Through these ritual signs some interpersonal relationship is established among those celebrating:
"There is only a sign if someone makes a sign to
another. . . . It always assumes an interpersonal activity with
the intent to communicate";[21] Second, liturgical signs and
symbols communicate *toward* those present as a means of
manifesting God's action and presence in our human life.
They evoke and call the assembled people into communion
with God beyond the reality of the sensible signs.

In the first level of communication—through the liturgical
signs *among* the assembled worshipers—the meaning and
value of symbolic activity needs to be attended to, taken seriously, and above all, engaged in with one's whole self,
because:

*Communication through symbolic signs is a complex act
which is addressed not only to the intellect but to the senses*

15

and to the imagination, to the will and to the heart, and finally, to one's freedom.[22]

Through this ensemble of signs and symbols, the worshiping community communicates *to* each other and *for* each other the "Mystery" present yet absent, revealed and yet hidden. This Mystery for the Christian is God in Christ reconciling the world to himself. All the elements of ritual activity in the liturgical assembly (e.g., art forms) serve to communicate to each member of the assembly the reality of the coming of God's Kingdom revealed in Christ. The symbols and signs of the rite are the best medium for humanly communicating this Mystery that is always greater than we are. Such symbolic activity

> . . . *produces meaning but also feeling. It affects self-awareness, wishes, and freedom. It invites you to take a stance.*[23]

Ritual activity for the liturgical assembly, then, fosters the inter-communication of those celebrating the event of God's enduring covenant with humankind.

In the second level of communication—*through* the liturgical signs—the emphasis is on God, whose love is communicated and revealed to us. These signs and symbols used by the worshiping community are called "sacred signs" because in faith the assembly recognizes and consents to the new and deeper meaning, (i.e., God's life and love in Christ) communicated through them.

> *It is God who makes a sign to the human person and communicates to that person. By these action-signs of the liturgy God sanctifies humanity . . . these signs are not only natural . . . but holy (communicating God's holiness) and "sacred."*[24]

In the liturgical assembly these "sacred signs" convey the "otherness," the "beyond," the "transcendent"—that which is not simply "of this world"—the "divine," the "totally other," the "holy." In whatever way one expresses this dimension of "sacredness" communicated through the signs used by the worshiping assembly, the point is that God desires to communicate God's very self to us. And for the Christian community, this "sacredness" is primarily in the humanity of Jesus, the Christ. All the "sacred signs" are intended, first of all, to communicate this final revelation of God in Christ Jesus to those who believe and gather for worship.

Gelineau speaks of three different senses of the "sacredness" of signs used in worship: a) to communicate the ultimate reality to which the sign or symbols refer (i.e., God); b) to communicate a particular religious meaning (e.g., the meal as a communion in the Body of Christ); and c) to communicate a particular usage that the believing community makes of certain words, gestures, or things (e.g., bread or music). Their "sacredness" is not *in* the things themselves but in the way believers make use of them to communicate God's revelation in the humanity of Christ.[25]

Hence, the liturgical assembly in all its ritual, symbolic activity—its "sacraments"—manifests on many levels and in different ways God's communication of God's self in Christ. To convey the height, depth, and breadth of this Mystery, many forms of human communication are employed and needed in worship. As Gelineau asserts:

> The liturgy is a parabolic type of activity (which throws us aside), metaphorical (which takes us somewhere else), allegorical (which speaks of something else) and symbolic (which brings together and makes connections. . . . Ritual activity is not concerned with producing purely "worldly" effects . . . but the coming of the Kingdom.[26]

However, in the communication through religious ritual, as in all human communication, there are certain factors or conditions that help or prevent this communication in the gathered assembly. Gelineau notes four that are significant: 1) the members of the assembly must know the *"code,"* that is, the system of meanings for the different sensible signs, if there is to be the desired communication in the rite; for example, the language spoken: "I can only understand a speaker if I know the language that he speaks or if someone translates his message for me in my own language."[27] This is essential for the liturgy because the word-language expresses the meaning of the rite.

2) The assembly must recognize the *context* in which different signs or symbols have their meaning and can be communicated intelligibly; for example, the color "white" can be a sign of joy or sorrow, depending on the context. For the assembly, two kinds of contexts must be attended to: a) the believers' surrounding culture, which is brought by them whenever they come to worship together (e.g., the arts, social customs, etc.); and b) the Gospel context, which is the distinguishing mark of the Christian assembly—namely, the revelation of God in the Judaic-Christian tradition. Without a sense of this context, the rites in Christian worship would not communicate much to those participating. The image, for example, "Lamb of God, you take away the sins of the world . . ." would not convey its depth of meaning without this Gospel context. Furthermore, this particular context of the Gospel gives new and deeper meaning to the words, gestures, and things that are borrowed from the surrounding cultural context for the purpose of worship. Each local liturgical assembly of Christians must be related to this Gospel context if genuine communication is to take place.

Without this understanding of these two kinds of contexts, the rites of the worshiping community can be confusing or simply misunderstood. Gelineau says:

> *Most misunderstandings or mistakes concerning the meaning of the rites in a celebration come, not from the inadequacy of this rite to its function, but from the absence of context or from the influence of another context which diverts the rite from its meaning.*[28]

3) A third factor that enters into the communication through ritual in the liturgical assembly is the unique and *personal experience* of each person in the assembly *as well as* the experience *common* to those worshiping. For example, if either the individuals or the group worshiping has never experienced raising one's hands for prayer, it will be more diffi-

cult for this sign to communicate anything. Metaphors and images will be all the more necessary to get in touch with the experiential element in individuals and in the group; e.g., a feeling of being drowned by one's work (cf, Ps. 69:2,3).

4) Finally, the psychological openness to symbolic consciousness is, perhaps, one of the most pressing factors for real communication and participation through ritual activity. Gelineau says:

> . . . People who are not accustomed to poetic, artistic, or musical language, or symbolic acts among their means of expression and communication find the liturgy like a foreign country, whose customs and language are strange to them.[29]

Without this psychological disposition to symbolic awareness in human communication, the rites of a worshiping community could be reduced to an explanatory and moralizing level. A liturgical assembly, reduced to this level of communication in its rites, will hardly meet the God of Jesus Christ as "the One-who-comes as the utterly new, the One who would never have restricted us within an ideology, or possessed us by a moral code."[30]

Ritual, then, is corporate symbolic activity. In the context of a Christian worshiping community, it is the medium of communication revealing the God in Christ, who is the ground and reality to which the ensemble of signs and symbols refer. This ensemble serves also to communicate to the participants of the assembly gathered in faith the meaning and content of their coming together. On both levels, the ritual activity (i.e., the ensemble of liturgical signs) is the means of communication of the Christ-event to and among the assembled worshiping community. To know what aids and what hinders the flow of communication through the ritual action allows the ritual to do its proper task: the communication of life, meaning, and value for the gathered worshipers.

An Assembly that Hears the Word of God and Breaks Bread Together

Indeed, why must Christians gather? First, to listen to the Word of God and to respond to it; and second, to give thanks and praise in celebrating the Lord's Supper.[31]

For the Christian Catholic community, the celebration of the Eucharist is the central worship activity where the reality of being a liturgical assembly is most frequently and commonly experienced. It is in this rite that the two basic elements of Christian worship are found—word and sacrament—forming the "model" structure for the celebration of God's covenant in Christ with the human family. This assembly at worship is formed by the proclamation of God's Word and is nourished by the Word who is the Bread of Life and the Cup of salvation through the sacramental action that follows the Word proclaimed.

Gelineau's theology of the liturgical assembly also involves his understanding of "the service or liturgy of the Word" and "the service or liturgy of the Meal" (the "breaking of bread," as it is called in the Acts of the Apostles 2:44). They are normally joined and experienced in the one eucharistic celebration by an assembly of worshipers. The eucharistic celebration is significant for an understanding of the liturgical assembly because a) each eucharistic celebration manifests the intimate connection between word and sacrament, and b) the eucharistic celebration is the sacrament of unity of the church and is the source of its life and mission during its pilgrimage toward the eternal banquet of the Kingdom.

In the first movement of the eucharistic celebration, the liturgy of the Word, the assembly listens and responds to the creative, redemptive, and sanctifying Word of God made flesh in Jesus Christ. In the liturgy of the Word, the assembly experiences anew the dialogue of love that God has begun with the human family. This exchange between God and the human family continues through the service of the Word and forms God's people here and now in this gathered worship community. Gelineau states as axiomatic: "There are no assemblies without the Word of God in dialogue with God's people."[32] From the origins of the liturgy of the Word in the Jewish synagogue and through its development in the early centuries of the Christian community, Gelineau finds a structure that is constant but flexible, containing the constitutive elements of this liturgy of the Word:

> We discover in a clear and constant manner throughout the different types of assemblies (e.g. the first part of the Sunday Mass, daily synaxes in the morning and evening, vigils for feasts or anniversaries of martyrs, pilgrim stations, etc.) the presence of four constitutive elements which we call the liturgy of the Word:
> 1. Readings from Scripture with homily;
> 2. Singing of psalms and hymns;
> 3. Prayer of the people;
> 4. Prayer of the presiding priest.[33]

Each element of this structure, and the inner dynamism of the whole, serves to form the gathered worshipers into a people rooted in faith, growing in hope, and living the love of God. Thus the proclamation of the Word (See 1 above) recalls the saving initiative of God in human history, gathering a people to be God's own, in order to make present and alive for this particular assembly that same mystery of God's love. Those assembled are invited to respond to this Word in faith (see 2 above), making this Word their own, through silent meditation and shared common song. But recognizing that the salvation offered in Christ Jesus is not yet attained, the assembly prays in its need that this salvation may become more a reality in this world (see 3 above). Finally, the assembly, through the ministry of its presiding celebrant, expresses and brings its prayer before the Father in union with and through the prayer of Christ Jesus who intercedes continually for us (see 4 above).

Although the liturgy of the Word in some sense "prepares" the assembly for the sacramental action that follows, Gelineau nonetheless insists that it must not be understood as a didactic or pedagogical moment that precedes the more mystical moment of the sacramental rite. This would be a distortion of the efficacious power of the Word of God among the assembly of worshipers. Rather, says Gelineau:

> *The celebration of the Word is already mystery. Since it is God who speaks to his people, the Lord is present there and acting through his Spirit in the heart of each person. The Word does not consist in words, song or preaching. The Word is Christ. Beyond the message addressed to the intelligence of the faithful, there is the One who speaks and who knocks at the door to enter and make his dwelling among us.* [34]

Thus, the service of the Word in the liturgical assembly already creates in the participants the salvation proclaimed through that Word, and realizes in a profound way here and now for this assembly the dialogue of love between God and God's people.

The liturgy of the Word moves into the liturgy of the Meal. All the wonders of God's love announced in the Word have their climax in the saving death and resurrection of Jesus. The eucharistic meal of Christians is the memorial of that saving activity in the symbol of a meal shared together. The night before he handed over his life, Jesus shared a last meal with his close friends. During that meal he told them that what he had done with them would be the sign by which to remember him as the New Covenant between God and the human family, and as the sign of that unity with him and his followers among themselves whenever they gathered in his name to share this memorial meal. Sharing this thanksgiving meal,

> *. . . the assembly of Christians does nothing more than obey the commandment of its Lord: 'Do this, in memory of me.'* [35]

The eucharistic meal, then, manifests and realizes in a special way Jesus' work and mission of gathering the dispersed children of the Father in order to give praise and thanks for God's faithful love, and, in the sharing of the one bread and cup, to bring about the unity of God's people in Christ.

As with the liturgy of the Word, so also the liturgy of the Meal is rooted in Jewish customs, but has been developed by the Christian community. Gelineau summarizes the "that" which Jesus did and told his disciples to do in memory of him at that final meal with them:

We come thus to *four* significant actions:
1. Taking the bread and wine;
2. Giving thanks;
3. Breaking the bread;
4. Distributing the bread and wine.[36]

The recalling of Jesus' words to "do this in memory of me" is inserted in that action of giving thanks to God over the bread and wine where the words express the whole work of salvation now being realized in this symbolic meal.

Those four actions of Jesus at the Last Supper form the outline of the church's eucharistic rite:

1. *Taking bread and wine:* the preparation of the bread and wine for the sacrifice of praise and thanksgiving;

3. *Giving thanks:* the eucharistic prayer, giving thanks for the work of our salvation, especially the death and resurrection and ascension of Jesus, and the calling down of the Holy Spirit upon the bread and wine and the assembly;

3. *Breaking the bread:* the breaking of the bread (and the pouring of the wine) for the participants of the meal, as the sign of unity in Christ;

4. *Distributing or giving the bread and wine:* the partaking of the body and blood of Christ in the bread and cup of wine.

Like the liturgy of the Word, the liturgy of the eucharistic meal serves the liturgical assembly by enabling it to show the unity of God's people in the body of Christ. The bread and wine for the thanksgiving sacrifice of the church (see 1 above) are brought forward from the assembly and are signs of all God's gifts to God's people. The worshipers express in this action their desire to return and surrender all to God and become one with the surrender and gift of Jesus in his saving death and resurrection. The prayer of blessing over the bread and wine (see 2 above), publicly proclaimed by the presiding celebrant presumes an assembly of worshipers who together remember with gratitude and praise the wonders of God's love in Christ, and pray for the fullness of the Kingdom. The breaking of the bread into many pieces (see 3 above) is a sign of unity in the one body of Christ to which all those assembled are called. Finally, the action of eating and drinking eucharistic food and drink (see 4 above) is the gesture by which the assembly symbolizes its communion with God and the members of the assembly with each other. This last action is the purpose and completion of the meal liturgy. The assembly of worshipers is then dissolved and sent forth in to the world to live out its love and unity in Christ.

Word and sacrament are essential to the worship of the Christian assembly. Through these two "liturgies" of the one eucharistic celebration, the assembly of worshipers is formed by the Word of God and is nourished by the same Word as the Bread of Life and the Cup of Salvation. Each part needs the other. As Gelineau expresses it:

> . . . the fruit of the sacrament depends on the degree of faith's involvement. Faith, however, deepens by the continual referring of life to the gospel. Inversely, every coming to the Word refers to the sacrament and makes the word efficacious.[37]

The liturgical assembly that hears and responds to God's Word and breaks bread together is the sign of the messianic banquet where God and God's people sit down and eat together in the intimacy of mutual friendship.

Summary:

Considerable time has been spent on Gelineau's understanding of the meaning of the liturgical assembly. It is the principal subject (the "we") of the liturgical actions. The self-image and self-understanding of the worshiping assembly is key and central to all that happens in the celebration of the liturgy. The assembly is a sign of the New Covenant in Christ Jesus. Its reality contains its own peculiar tensions and polarities. It is the center of the communication through signs and symbols with God and others. It is the assembly who hears and responds to the Word. It is the partaker in the Meal of the Lord. Because the reality of the liturgical assembly—

God's people gathered for worship here and now—is so fundamental, all the rites, gestures, actions, and objects pertaining to the worship activity function within, and for the sake of, this assembly. Liturgy is for the sake of the people and not the people for the sake of the liturgy.

According to Gelineau, an understanding of music in Christian worship, must be sought in the context of our understanding of the liturgical assembly. Music has its own meaning apart from Christian worshiping assemblies. Gelineau would surely admit this. But when music is employed in the context of the Christian liturgical assembly, it contains a specific theological dimension and meaning that is related to the reality of the liturgical assembly.

Chapter 2

Music as a Constitutive Element in Christian Worship

Christian assemblies have at all times and in all places read the Scriptures, prayed, and sung. The Christian liturgy was born singing, and it has never ceased to sing. . . . Singing . . . must be regarded as one of the fundamental constituents of Christian worship. . . . The Church used music and singing in its worship well before it began to ask itself questions about why and wherefore. . . .[1]

Chapter one dealt with Gelineau's understanding of "l'assemblée liturgique" (the liturgical assembly) as the subject, the agent of all the liturgical gestures, words, signs, and actions performed in the celebration. "Pas de liturgies sans assemblée"—without an assembly of faith, there is no liturgical action. Music and its theological meaning in the worship of the Christian assembly will be the focus of this chapter. Certain questions will guide the investigation into Gelineau's writings, such as: How does music "speak" in worship? What does music "mean" theologically in the Christian assembly of worship? Is music a mere decoration for the worship activity? Is music present in worship to give aesthetic pleasure? Does the presence of music in worship merely justify and affirm the religious value of art? What is the distinctive theological meaning of music in Christian worship?

The renewal and revival of singing and music in the Christian Catholic liturgy during the past twenty-five years or so (just before and after the Second Vatican Council, 1962-1965), indicates a deeper meaning in the use of song and instruments for the Christian worshiping assembly. Gelineau holds that the theological meaning of music for worship lies in its ability and power to express and deepen the religious experience of those assembled for worship.[3] Music possesses the power to embody and realize the communion and communication in faith and love of those assembled to worship. Music strengthens and symbolizes, by its own particular dynamism, our eschatological communion in the Lord. The use and choice of music for the liturgical assembly becomes, then, a question of what is most meaningful or valuable for communicating and deepening the event of God's love in Jesus Christ here and now in this worshiping assembly. It is not simply a matter of what is most beautiful or what is aesthetically pleasing. These dimensions are not completely irrelevant, but they are not the essential point to music in worship. Music is theologically meaningful for worship because it can express and deepen the reality of God's Mystery in Christ for the assembled worshipers. As Gelineau asserts:

> In order that a sung rite function as such, it is not enough that the piece (of music) be practical, or that it works, or that everyone is singing, or that the music be beautiful. It is necessary that, by the song and music, Jesus Christ be present and acting in the assembly, that his Word be proclaimed and lived, that communion in his Spirit be realized.[4]

The guiding principle or theological meaning of the music for worship will consist in how it can help to deepen and develop among the members of the worshiping assembly the awareness of the Paschal Mystery that this assembly celebrates. The particular style or repertoire of the music for worship will take account of the assembly celebrating here and now. The theological significance of the music in the worship context will be grounded in its intimate relation to the liturgical assembly, as it celebrates the New Covenant in word and sacrament. Music gives a meaning to the worship by its service to the liturgical assembly, inviting and affirming this group of worshipers in greater faith, hope, and love of the mystery of Jesus Christ. The music of worship, as do all other signs and symbols of the assembly, communicates the Mystery of God's presence to this worshiping assembly, uniting it more deeply to its creator as source and to one another in God. The sounds we hear in the music of worship should lead us to surrender in faith and love to what is unheard.

Gelineau states what music brings to the liturgical celebration:

I am personally convinced that music can bring to the celebration something else which is quite peculiar to music. In the same way that icons ought to make us contemplate the invisible, music ought make us hear what is unheard . . . this music . . . so transparent to that which it celebrates that it would be an inexhaustible source of prayer, of meaning, of affections. . . . Music, not filled with itself, but a carrier of silence and adoration, as the Virgin Mary was for the Word of God. [5]

Therefore, in Gelineau's writings, music has theological significance in worship because it holds a symbolic power to communicate the mystery of God's love to the assembled believers. Because it completes the meaning of the word and actions of the worshiping assembly, music is a constitutive element of the liturgical celebration. Its functional meaning is, then, to embody and enrich the different ritual moments in the assembly's worship. Three aspects of Gelineau's thinking on music in worship will guide us:

1) Music as symbol;
2) Music as constitutive element;
3) Music as it functions in the Eucharistic Prayer.

1) *Music as Symbol*

As soon as we gather, as soon as we celebrate, a certain music is already there—in the resonance of the sanctuary, be it delightful, or annoying; it is in the timbre of a voice, pleasant or unpleasant; it's in the collective murmur of a crowd reciting a prayer. . . . Music is also in the diaphragms of the loudspeakers; in the vibrations of bells. . . . It takes very little to hinder prayer; but it takes but a single beautiful sound to exalt it. [6]

The question that Gelineau frequently asks is: What do singing and music communicate to the worshiping Christian assembly? What meaning is conveyed through singing and music in worship that is different and unique and not reducible to something else? He approaches this question through the notion of symbolic communication. In the previous chapter, I quoted Gelineau concerning the importance of an openness to symbolic consciousness.[7] The symbol, as medium of communication, is essential to Christian worship. Music—primarily song, but also instrumental sounds—is, in Gelineau's view, one of the most fundamental and ordinary symbolic expressions communicating various levels of meaning in the assembly at worship. The presence and importance of this medium of meaning would be clearly verified if one reviewed the history of music in worship.[8]

How, then, is music a symbolic form in Christian worship? And what does it symbolize? First of all, Gelineau distinguishes a symbol from a signal, and a sign, in the strict sense. A signal, like a military bugle call, is a indication to do something, or of something happening. A sign in the strict sense, like a barbershop pole, ordinarily conveys a univocal meaning.[9] A symbol, on the other hand, always contains in itself a plurality of meanings, an excess of meaning. It can have many meanings on a variety of levels, as, for example, the symbol of water. This can symbolize bathing or drowning, or both at once; it can indicate coolness, life, or destruction. It cannot be reduced to a single meaning. It is a mistake

> ... to think that "the" meaning of symbol can be explained. . . . It is not like a word whose meaning can be looked up in the dictionary. It is an inexhaustible source of possible new meanings. Hence its richness.[10]

Second, the meaning of symbol is not confined to its intellectual content; it adds the affective, feeling element as well as an invitation to practical action. Thus, it affects our self-consciousness, our desires, our freedom. It challenges us to take a stance in our life situation. The authentic symbol has the nature of combining, of throwing together many elements into a whole. A symbol that communicates humanly, contains the bodily, affective, intellectual, and volitional dimensions. As a form of communication, a symbol

> turns me upside down, provokes me, forces me to adopt a

position before it, before myself, before others. The symbol is the field where the story of our free expression is acted out.[11]

Symbols in Christian worship are perceptible realities—what is seen, said, done, heard, felt, smelled—that point to another reality, to what is "beyond" the sensible reality. They are intended to arouse faith, hope, and love for the dynamic presence of the risen Christ and for the coming of God's kingdom in our world. Music, in the context of the Christian assembly's worship, is one of the symbolic forms that points to and communicates the inner reality of what is being done by the assembly at worship.

Even before its use in the worship context of Christians, music is a symbolic form that points beyond itself. From the myriad of sounds in nature, like the song of birds, the whistling of the wind, the crash of waves, etc., human beings create music to express a new meaning, an interpretation of the world of sounds in nature. A musical creation "humanizes" these natural sounds in the effort to express meaning through the arrangement of different sounds. According to Gelineau, music is symbolic in a primary sense because it is an art form. He formulates his understanding of art thus:

> *If the artist is not content with nature as it is, that is because he has in mind some other order of beauty. He is trying to interpret the most profound yearning which is inscribed in the heart of man: to discover the world which lies beyond this visible world. . . . Man aspires to the eternal. He tends to fashion for himself that which nothing in the whole world displays to him. So the artist takes possession of nature in order to make it express something which it is not. . . . And so, by rhythm and cadence, the poet pretends that his words bring into existence the substance of what they express. The dancer portrays a new mode of existence, entirely free. The painter gives form and color to the invisible, and the musician, in the sonorous language of sound evolved by his own spirit, speaks of realities which transcend speech.*[12]

But, for those who believe in the Word of God become flesh, music symbolizes the presence and reality of the New Creation in Christ Jesus—the kingdom of God. The opening of our ears to faith enables believers to hear the sounds of creation differently and, in that faith, create music that speaks and points to this New Creation. The assembly at worship is the sign of this kingdom present already in the world through the gathering and celebration of faith. Because of the Word-made-flesh, the full meaning of human song and music is revealed: God, the source and creator of all things, is praised eternally through the faithful and perfect love offered by the Word, the first-born of all creation. It is this truth, Gelineau asserts, " . . .which ever continues to resound in the songs of Christian liturgy."[13]

Music, as employed in the context of the Christian assembly of worship, builds on the human dimensions of all song and instrumental music. Music expresses meaning through its power of feeling, affectivity, and intensity. It adds the non-utilitarian, purposeless element. It can help create community in the union of voices in song. It expresses celebration and festival in human life. The effect of music in an assembly of worship is brought about because of the symbolic power of music to "linger over the words, touch the heart, lay open the mystery, give the feeling of festive enjoyment."[14]

Because the liturgical assembly is the sign of the New Creation in Christ, its music is the expression of Jesus' own worship and love together with his people. The thanksgiving and praise of the church, its pleading, its pondering the Word of God, its desire for unity, are all done in and through Christ Jesus. The music of the worship contains the power of communicating the full extent and depth of these movements of prayer in and through Christ. Each of these movements of prayer in the context of the liturgy is rooted in human experiences that are transformed and expressed in musical form to heighten and bring out the "new" meaning in Christ. For example, a song of pleading or supplication in the texts, "Lord, have mercy," "Save us, O God," is rooted in the human cry for help. In the worship context, it symbolizes the assembly's cry for salvation and liberation in Christ. Or, to take another example, the human experience of joy, love, or gratitude is transformed and expressed in the music and song of praise and thanksgiving in the texts, "O give thanks to the Lord for he is good," "Alleluia!" For the worshiper, the song and music expressing this experience symbolizes the wholeness, the freedom, the gift of being children of God in the Son. The community of faith in Christ, aware of God's goodness and gift of love, breaks forth in a joyful sound to the Lord (cf. Ps. 81:2,3).

The worship of the liturgical assembly is fundamentally a shared, communal action. Music in worship can express this communal dimension, this sense of unity and oneness in Christ, in a unique way. A sense of belonging and being united to something larger than one's individual world is communicated through the power of the music performed together in worship. A diversity of individuals with different backgrounds, histories, and temperaments, can become united through the song and music of the liturgy. It has the power of removing barriers between people. It can create and strengthen bonds between people of diverse interests and talents. It symbolizes the *koinonia*, the fellowship of believers in Christ.

Gelineau expresses this dimension of the symbolic power of music in worship when he says:

> *Many individual voices . . . can actually be fused together, so that when they blend and follow the same rhythm, only one voice is heard—that of the group. This brings out a very strong feeling of unity and of belonging. It even touches on the essential mystery of the church as* **koinonia.** *From the time of Antioch down to our own day, singing with one voice has remained a privileged way of expressing unity in diversity.*[15]

Furthermore, singing and music symbolize the aspect of festival for the Christian community at worship. The liturgical assembly is the sign of the festive gathering of God's redeemed people (Heb. 12:22ff; Rev. 14, 15). It is unthinkable to have a festival without singing, music, and even dancing. The believing, worshiping community in Christ symbolizes, in its musical outpouring, the joy and love of a people redeemed by the Lamb. It sings a "new song" to the Lamb and to the One who sits on the throne (Rev. 5:9-14). The Eucharist celebrated by the assembly of believers is a sacrifice of praise anticipating the festival of the kingdom that is to come. It is a sign, Gelineau says, that "needs singing if the sign is to be complete."[16] Singing and music in Christian worship symbolize a fullness, a completion already present in some way in the festive worship of the Christian community.

Thus, the symbolic nature of music in the worship activity of the gathered believers consists, in Gelineau's view, in its ability to manifest what is happening on a deeper level. It carries many meanings; it communicates depth, power, intensity, and warmth to the celebrating assembly. But the fundamental meaning of song and music for the worship of the Christian assembly is that this gift of God to humankind

> . . . *might signify the suffering and glory, the sacrifice and love of his Son who dies and lives among his brethren. It is a mystery of faith. But because it is a sign it is not the reality itself.*[17]

Music in worship is a symbol because of its excess and plurality of meanings. It both reveals and hides. It expresses what is present and what it absent. It is both sound and silence. In the music used by the liturgical assembly, Gelineau holds that the key question is: "What are we signifying to each other, to people outside the group, in doing what we do? Are we just celebrating ourselves or is it the God of Jesus Christ whom we proclaim, petition, and praise? Does our music make us hear something other than itself?"[18] Music for Christian worship becomes symbolic because it is part of the symbolic value of the worshiping assembly. For this liturgical assembly has Jesus Christ as its center. In the power of his Spirit, the worshipers are caught up in the love and surrender of Jesus to the Father. Song and music in this assembly express, deepen, and communicate more effectively the multidimensional meaning of why we worship as Christians. Music in the context of worship cannot rest in itself, however pleasing or beautiful. It always points beyond itself, to the One we worship as we gather together as God's people.

In a lyric passage, Gelineau expresses his deepest theological meaning of music for worship:

> Music can never reveal to us the whole of its mystery until it has become silent and no more sounds reach our ears. For the praise of heaven, pure love, will have no further need for the art of sound. After this life the only music which will be able to satisfy the soul will be the music of silence! . . . He who sings with faith must never allow himself to be immersed in the mere delight of musical sounds or yield himself to the euphony of cadence; for through music he is searching for that which no ear has ever heard. Rhythm and melos are like a pair of wings which carry him up to the point where he will hear something else: the single note, anterior to all time, wherewith the Word of God praises the Father in the Spirit of love.[19]

2) *Music as Constitutive Element of the Liturgical Celebration*

> Music . . . is not of the essence of liturgy . . . but it enters into the rite as a constitutive element of the normal and perfect form of the word in the liturgy. . . . Thus, although music is not of itself to be considered as a rite, song is in fact a "part" of the liturgy in the same way as reading or prayer; it is, moreover, a part necessary to the integrity of the rites . . .[20]

In Gelineau's view, music in Christian worship carries deep symbolic meaning and value for the liturgical assembly. The worship of the church in all its actions, words, gestures, and symbols is celebrated by, and on behalf of, the liturgical assembly. Those who worship together participate in the saving mystery of Jesus Christ. The music of worship, or liturgical music, is done, likewise, by and on behalf of the assembly of worship. At worship, music is a personal activity whereby each and all the participants share in the Event being celebrated, namely, the New Covenant in Jesus Christ.

Music is symbolic in the context of Christian worship. But it is also constitutive. It forms an integral part of the liturgical action of the assembly. Music is constitutive because it contributes part of the full meaning of the ritual actions done by the assembled worshipers. By this, Gelineau means that music for worship is not something accessory or superfluous. The presence of music accompanies the various ritual actions of the whole service and brings an added dimension to each of the ritual actions and to the totality of the worship service.

One of Gelineau's basic convictions concerning music for worship is that this music is an act of prayer, an act of worship done in a particular worship service by a specific assembly. Liturgical music is not primarily the repertoire or style of music, for repertoire and style of music must be related to the actual worship of a celebrating assembly. Liturgical music is a creative act of prayer and worship within a structure. It is an event within something ready-made. Worship music exists or is most real only when believers actually make music for this or that particular liturgy both in its distinctive ritual moments and as a totality. Music brings, therefore, an element of newness within the context of a structured, formal, and repetitive rite. Gelineau expresses this when he says:

> Music . . . is never simply "something done, once for all." It always needs to be redone, reinterpreted, re-created. It can only exist when someone makes it. Music, like the rite, is both repetition and innovation. All its evocative power rests in the fruitful interplay of these two aspects.[21]

Music in the liturgical tradition has never completely lost its creative quality in the worship context. Liturgical texts were prescribed but they have been expressed in many different musical settings. Even the performance of a musical work is never exactly the same for each liturgical celebration. And finally, improvisation on the organ during the liturgy has never entirely disappeared. Music constitutes a part of the total meaning of the ritual actions by its power to express anew, through the art of sound, the purpose and meaning of the ritual words and actions.

Rite, or liturgy, or the ensemble of ritual actions and words is not mere ceremonial. There is a stability and a repetitiveness in an established liturgy. But Christian liturgy must also possess the element of newness, innovation:

. . . Even if the rite is laid down, it is like an inner model of a meaningful act whose form must constantly be reinvented or modified. Even if the rite is by nature "repetitive" it is never pure repetition. At the level of the realities of the faith, the liturgy is always newness, New Covenant, paschal renewal. So shouldn't something of this newness be shown at the level of signs? New being and new appearance are inseparable.[22]

In the present stage of liturgical renewal, liturgical forms in the churches of the liturgical tradition are more flexible than formerly. Gelineau suggests that the ritual forms used in the worship service need to be seen as "operational models"[23] rather than as fixed, immutable and lifeless entities that work of and by themselves without any intervening human creativity. Gelineau defines this concept of a working model in liturgy:

What I call "the operational model" is the received capacity of reproducing an expressive and meaningful way of behaving based on a pattern and taking into account differences of time, place, people and the available abilities and resources. The eucharistic prayer in the Apostolic Tradition . . . a model . . . a psalm-tone is a formula-model; . . . the structure of the Liturgy of the Word . . . is a rite-model. A model can be applied to separate rites or to ritual sequences. It is both fidelity in substance and the life of the forms bearing meaning.[24]

Music in liturgy is one of those signs/symbols through which the new element, the creative expression, is brought to the liturgical celebration as a whole and to the separate ritual moments within it. Whatever the musical form used in worship, it must be related intrinsically to the ritual forms. Music—song and instrument—enlivens, brings a new life to the ritual forms. Through the language of music, the inner meaning of the ritual forms is heightened and revealed. When music is employed in worship in its relationship to the different ritual moments, a dilemma—music as a purely artistic work versus the act of worship—is avoided and solved through musical expression of the rites. Gelineau's option is clear. Music communicates a fuller meaning to the ritual forms by its creative expression. Music, unconnected with the ritual forms of the worship service, could be "music for its own sake." For Gelineau, liturgical music derives its theological meaning from the fact that it is a creative expression and a new dimension to the ritual forms that comprise the whole liturgy:

> Music . . . gets its meaning from the celebration as a whole, provided that it in some way prepares for, accompanies, or prolongs the word and the sacrament. It is as signs of, and for, faith that singing and music enter into the sacramental economy of Christian worship. [25]

The liturgies of word and sacrament are the two fundamental rites of Christian worship. Through them, when celebrated in faith, the assembly of worshipers is formed as God's people, sign of the New Covenant in Christ. When these rites are clothed, or expressed musically, the full force and depth of these rites touch the worshipers affectively and interiorly, and thus communicate the newness of God's revelation of love in Christ. The liturgy of the Word is the proclamation of, and the response to, the saving love of God in Jesus Christ. Each liturgical assembly has to create a musical expression of this rite that will clearly unfold and complete the spoken word because, Gelineau's states, ". . . song . . .as a flowering of the spoken language . . . is word in the fullest sense." [26]

The liturgy of the sacrament of Eucharist is both the public praise and thanksgiving for God's wonderful deed of love and the meal of communion with the Lord. The particular celebrating assembly expresses these actions of praise, supplication, and communion also through music, revealing the festive and social character of these actions. Music, when constitutive of the ritual forms in worship, expresses and communicates even more, therefore, the meaning of the realities symbolized by the ritual words and ritual actions.

The distinctive meaning of liturgical music, then, is not simply in the beauty of the music but in *how* it is the activity of those personally participating in the liturgy and how fully it enters into the ritual action; "whereas," Gelineau says, "the more it becomes an esthetic entity tending to be a manifestation of human culture in its own right, the less suited it is for use in worship."[27] Music for worship has a theological meaning because it is constitutive of the ritual forms of the assembly's worship. Music plays an integral part in manifesting, expressing, and communicating the purpose and meaning of the individual ritual moments of the liturgy as well as in revealing the tone and character of the whole liturgy. For example:

> . . . a very simple tune can be dismissed as worthless if taken in isolation but makes a marvelous contribution to the spirit and beauty of the celebration, whereas a great work which is too difficult or badly done can wreck it.[28]

The theological meaning of song and music in worship consists in its being a particular sign, means, or channel for celebrating the Mystery of God's love in this specific liturgical assembly. Music offers to the worship activity—in its individual parts and as a totality—what Gelineau calls an "outil célébratoire" (a celebrational instrument).[29] As an example, the music for an acclamation, for a psalm, or for the Lord's prayer, brings something more into existence that did not exist before. Such music enables the liturgical assembly to join together in an act of celebration—a shared, communal activity. Music has the power to evoke and communicate this social and celebrational aspect of the liturgy in a unique way.

Furthermore, as an "outil célébratoire," music, when employed in different worship contexts and with different kinds of liturgical assemblies, will express the meaning of the rites in distinctive ways. For example, music for an important feast or special day will demand its own quality of expression. Music, for festive days, adds its meaning to the ritual activities in quite a different way. On these occasions:

> . . . we expect something more sumptuous: good tunes, moving harmonies, catching rhythms and a sound to fill the space. . . . On certain important days, flat, feeble tunes would be a disappointment. On these days we need

polyphony, instruments, larger works. People would also like to recognize them, hear well-known music which symbolizes the feast for them, as in the past . . . the Exsultet at Easter.[30]

Music for worship, in Gelineau's view, is constitutive of the celebration by the liturgical assembly because it adds a creative, new dimension to the individual ritual movements of the liturgy and to the celebration as a whole. Music enhances and liberates, unfolds and reveals the depth and inner meaning of the ritual activities. It expresses and communicates for the assembled worshipers, through its own unique art form, the Mystery of God's love in Christ, which is revealed, but still hidden, in the presence and activity of the liturgical assembly of God's people.

Gelineau clearly states his conviction of the intimate relationship of rite and music:

Each time that music occurs in the liturgy, it does so in order to fulfill a ritual function. Sometimes, it accompanies the rite while being integrated with it more or less closely, sometimes, it even constitutes the rite.[31]

Music is constitutive of the liturgical celebration because it is symbolic. It expresses and communicates a meaning to those assembled. Thus, music has theological meaning in worship because it serves the celebrating assembly in expressing more fully its ritual activities. Music in worship can never be an end in itself, it is only a means—important and integral—to the growth of faith, hope and love of the liturgical assembly. When the good, the well-being, and the deepening of faith in the assembled believers is primary and fundamental, then, Gelineau states:

It is the surest way the celebration has a living face, meaningful and personalised, especially when it concerns music and song.[32]

3) *Music in the Eucharistic Prayer*

In the *Constitution on the Sacred Liturgy* of Vatican II, music for worship is called a "ministerial function . . . in the service of the Lord."[33] Gelineau understands the function of music in worship to be more than a question of mere practicality or of a task to be fulfilled in the liturgy, (e.g., an opening song or instrumental work to begin the worship). It is rather the "*symbolic* function which opens up a space and freedom for the heart of the believer."[34] Music functions in this way very concretely and specifically according to resources, possibilities, and limitations of the celebrating assembly. Music is functional for worship when a particular piece of music attempts to express for this assembly the deepest meaning of the whole celebration or one of its ritual moments.

In this section, one specific ritual action—the eucharistic prayer—will be taken as an example of how Gelineau understands music functioning within the Christian liturgy.[35] The eucharistic prayer is the public prayer of praise and thanks of the assembled believers as they remember the wonderful works of God in creation and human history, and above all, the saving death-resurrection-ascension of Jesus Christ. In the context of this praise, and flowing from it, the assembly calls on God to send the promised Holy Spirit, and petitions God for the coming of fullness of the kingdom in our world. This prayer is the church's ritualization of Jesus' action of giving thanks at the Last Supper. It is the center of the liturgy of the Meal.[36]

The importance of using song and music for this ritual moment is clearly affirmed by Gelineau:

> *To speak of song as it relates to the Eucharist is not a question of what is "accessory." The Eucharist is a prayer of praise: the full expression of human praise is in song. The Eucharist is a festive meal: but singing is a privileged sign of festivity. The Eucharist is above all a spiritual sacrifice: but the activity of singing is a living image of the one who hands oneself over and, by voice and exhaled breath, goes toward the one he admires and loves.*[37]

This thanksgiving prayer proclaims God's eternal love in a poetic expression of grateful remembering, invocation, petition, and praise through Jesus Christ. As ritual sign, it should communicate its reality to the assembled believers. It is this celebrating assembly that is the "subject," the "we" that is doing the praying. The assembly needs to participate personally and actively in this central prayer of its worship. New efforts, therefore, are being made to use music effectively in order to communicate to the assembly the richness and depth of this public prayer.[38]

Gelineau, from his experience as pastor and animator of liturgical assemblies, suggests three formats for the use of music in the eucharistic prayer:

1) Acclamations within the prayer;
2) Opening song to the thanksgiving prayer;
3) Hymns integrated into the prayer;

1) *Acclamations:* These are short, musical "shouts" of praise, thanks, joy or petition, such as "Amen," "Alleluia," "Hosanna in the highest," "We bless and thank You, Lord." These sung acclamations punctuate the eucharistic prayer at the appropriate moments and ensure the active participation of the whole assembly. These musical pieces would function as emphasizing the proclamatory and poetic nature of this prayer. A distribution of these acclamations might go like this:

a) as a response to the introductory part of the prayer (the preface): Hosanna in the highest!
b) during the commemoration of salvation history: Blessed is he who comes in the Name of the Lord!
c) after the words of institution: Amen!
d) during the intercessions: Remember, Lord, your mercy!
e) as a conclusion to the whole prayer: Amen! Amen! Amen!

2) *Opening Song to the thanksgiving prayer:* This format suggests using a few stanzas of an appropriate hymn of praise and thanksgiving or a psalm with a refrain. The function of this music would be to invite the assembly to a mood of praise and thanksgiving as they begin this important ritual action. Gelineau parallels the function of this invitational song of praise to that of the opening song of a worship service. The value of this introduction to the eucharistic prayer is:

. . . to clearly mark from the beginning (as it is traditional for the eucharistic prayer) its festive and lyric quality. This is done so that the assembly becomes an involved member in the prayer of praise.[40]

This hymn or psalm of praise would lead immediately into the prayer led by the leader of the assembly. The prayer would also be interspersed with the usual, prescribed acclamation: the Sanctus (Holy, Holy, Holy Lord); the memorial acclamation; the final Amen.

A example of such an invitational song of praise would be: *Arise, come to your God. Sing him your songs of rejoicing (Refrain).*

The verses of Psalm 100 are then used:

Cry out to the Lord, all the earth;
Serve the Lord with gladness,
Come before him, singing for joy. . .

3) *Hymns integrated into the prayer:* In this format, appropriate stanzas of a hymn, expressing the mood and content of the eucharistic prayer, are integrated within the very structure of the prayer itself. A musical background can serve to unify the spoken, prescribed text and the stanzas of the hymn being used. Gelineau cites an example from the French-speaking repertoire:

(Sung between the initial dialogue and the preface):

In fullest voice we sing to God
Our songs of joy, our festive hymns!

(Sung during the preface, after the recalling of the mystery of the incarnation):

Think not that God in silence stays
When he has spoken through his birth.

(Sung before the invocation of the Holy Spirit over the bread and wine):

To announce the new creation
Let us take the bread of his tenderness.

(Sung after the prayer for unity):

Nothing at all can separate us
From the love and friendship of our God.[41]

In each of these formats, the function of the music in this ritual action is to serve the liturgical assembly in praying, fully and actively, its praise and thanksgiving to God. One cannot use such musical expressions for the eucharistic prayer as a novelty or a gimmick; instead, ''The changes should be motivated toward the good of the asembly and suggested as a way for the assembly to enter more deeply into the action and prayer of thanksgiving.''[42] In these concrete musical examples for the eucharistic prayer, Gelineau illustrates how his theology of music in worship works pastorally for the deepening of faith, hope and love in the assembled worshipers.

PART II
Erik Routley

Chapter 3:
The Word and the Gathered Congregation

*. . . The secret of the recovery of worship in the Reformed churches is . . . the recovery of the notion of the **gathered congregation** as prophet or folk artist. In other words, "would that all the Lord's people were prophets"; would that corporately they could recapture the skill, wisdom, discernment and gift for communication that the prophets of Israel had.*[1]

Erik Routley, the second representative for a theology of music in worship, comes from the Reformed, free-church tradition; in particular, the Congregational Church in England and Wales. In this tradition, the Word of God, as proclaimed and preached in the congregational worship, is central. In order to understand Routley's theology of music in worship, it is necessary to explore his understanding of the Word of God and its communication to humankind. For Routley, God's Word, as communicated to us in the words of the sacred writings of the Old and New Testaments, gives us the shape, the direction, and existential challenge in every aspect of church life, including that of church music. Because Scripture is concerned with communicating the ultimate truth and good of human life, its message and invitation to a fullness of life ground the meaning of every dimension of our personal and communal lives. The orientations, the principles, and the direction for full human living can be discovered in Scripture through its Spirit-led reading and meditation and preaching within the church.[2] In his short but substantial work, *Into a Far Country*, Routley says:

*For the Lord who speaks through the Bible speaks a Word which is of covenant, that is, of conversation. The Lord speaks to all humanity, and speaks in a love which **respects**.*

47

The whole testimony of Scripture, crowned by the living testimony of the ministry of Christ from Bethlehem to Pentecost, insists on this. The Author of the Word is asking not for the pupil's "yes" or the slave's "yes," but the existential "YES!" of the reborn son.[3]

In his theology of music for worship, Routley refers to its ground in the Word of God and its manner of communication to us. And what happens in the gathered congregation, its pattern and shape as it were, can be found rooted in the shape and pattern of God's Word expressed in Sacred Scripture. I will, therefore, cluster his reflections thus:

1) The Word of God and the images of trajectory and conversation; and

2) Free-church worship and the images of trajectory and conversation.

1) *The Word of God and the Images of Trajectory and Conversation*

Sacred Scripture is the written testimony of believers to the reality of God's Word revealed and active in the world. But Sacred Scripture also expresses the way God communicates his Word and love to the human family and thereby forms a people as God's own. In these sacred writings, there is an image of God that is communicated, according to Routley, in a "parabolic" way, not by a direct, exhaustive, systematic means. The Gospels—the life, ministry, death and resurrection of Jesus—in a particular fashion, exemplify the parabolic method of communicating the reality of God in Jesus. Jesus often spoke in parables to the people, and even when he did not speak in parables, there was a parabolic element to his words and teaching.[4] That is, he always left room, space for the hearer to respond—to interpret and apply—out of his or her own existential situation. Routley believes that this parabolic pattern, in the Gospels especially, reveals a basic understanding of God's way of communicating to humankind, thus giving us a more balanced image of the God of Scripture.

This parabolic pattern is transposed by Routley into the image "trajectory"[5] to express the kind of communication between God and the human family that Jesus, as the Word-made-flesh, was continually trying to make his hearers understand. Routley describes this image clearly when he says:

"Trajectory" is . . . the path described by the Word of God . . . between its leaving its source and its fruitfully lodging in the mind and heart of the believer. It is our contention here that all God's commands to the world are by trajectory. . . .[6]

This image evokes another, very ordinary experience, that of throwing a ball into the air for someone to catch. This is in contrast with the image of someone being passed a ball very securely so as to avoid dropping it. This contrast, for Routley, expresses the difference between two quite distinct images of God. In the trajectory image, God's life and will is communicated to us in a way that does not intervene so directly that it denies our human freedom or dignity. God speaks to us as we are listening and reaching out to God at the same time. This kind of divine love and respect for the human creature contains the element of "withdrawal, reticence, an avoidance of exhaustiveness"[7] and "respect,"[8] and allows the human response of love to be a real and indispensable partner in the process of the divine-human friendship. This kind of God always calls for an existential faith response whenever God's Word is addressed to the human partner(s) in mutual friendship.[9] This image, then, affirms both God's sovereign freedom and human freedom in the dialogue of love that permeates the pages of Scripture. The image of trajectory that Routley discovers in the scriptural Word of God tells of a God who, though infinitely greater than we, nevertheless desires and delights in our free (though frail at times) response of love to God's initiative.

A second image—conversation—is closely allied to that of trajectory in Routley's theology. Whereas "trajectory" brings out the aspect of God's Word as source—beyond us, yet communicating with us—the image of "conversation" emphasizes the aspect of response from free subjects to the Word of God. That God converses with the human family is not new. In fact, ". . . the notion that God's communication with men is by conversation . . . is as old as the story of Adam and Eve."[10]

And furthermore, in all the Old Testament figures, for example that of Moses (Ex. 33:18-23), or Isaiah (Is. 6), or Job (passim), one can find this conversation present, though in varying ways. God's mystery breaks into the world of human beings. God's Word seeks a response in the heart of the believer, so that this Word does not return empty (Is. 55:11). This image of conversation, like that of trajectory, reveals God's way of revealing God's self to the human family in a way that affirms God's mystery as inexhaustible and yet utterly respectful of the one to whom God's Word is spoken. In the Old Testament, the distance between the source and the human responder in this conversation, or within this trajectory, seems great, too great at times. But what of the New Covenant in Jesus? Routley asks. How is the image of conversation found?

With the incarnation of God in Jesus Christ, God became fully a part of our human lives and history. God has spoken to the human family, and still speaks to us, in Jesus, the son, the Word-made-flesh, in a way that does not impose itself. God's rule in Christ, even if more intimate to us, does not tyrannize us. God's will is not imposed on human beings even though God's coming in the humanity of the Son has clearly and definitively affirmed the faithful and everlasting love of God for us and our history. There is still space, "reticence and respect," present in this new conversation in Christ, so that tyranny of any kind is clearly not part of the Gospel message. Routley insists on this when he states:

> *Jesus Christ removed our anxiety; but he did not declare the end of the divine reticence. . . . It is the failure to observe that the divine reticence is not abrogated by the Incarnation and the coming of the Holy Spirit that has caused so much religious error and so much religious tyranny in history. The*

truth that Scripture and the record of Christ's life proclaim is very different from that. It declares to us in a less ambiguous fashion than any other authority to which we might commit ourselves what is the way in which we should treat one another, and how we should expect to hear the Word of God.[11]

Jesus' coming among us has not put an end to the way God communicates to us through trajectory and conversation. How, then, is this image of conversation verified in the New Testament? Routley compares the divine-human conversation, as expressed in the Scriptures, with human conversation. The kind of conversation that is found in God's communication with us in the scriptural word is one that avoids "mere instruction or mere information."[12] As in human conversation, mere instruction—how or what to do—can destroy responsibility and respect for the other. It lacks courtesy. Mere information stifles or does not wait for the question of the listener. It is bad pedagogy. But the dynamic of good human conversation is artful and is much more than instructing or informing. It humanizes, liberates, and delights both conversants.

But it is a process that demands for its fulfillment a certain degree of maturity. Conversation of the best kind does resemble two or three people sending one another rather difficult catches with a ball, each in turn throwing, the other catching and returning it, at a fairly high speed. In good conversation, every participant is alert to what the others are saying, and to some extent anticipates it. Yet at every moment each is immediately adaptable, so that each new turn, each new point made, finds him ready to receive it.[13]

Delight, laughter, joy—sometimes only in the form of a smile or chuckle—is characteristic of good human conversation. It is an unmistakable "sign of the apprehension of trajectory."[14]

The joy or blessedness proclaimed in the Gospels (Cf. Mt. 5) is the quality most characteristic of the New Testament kind of conversation, not unlike the kind of delight of catching a thrown ball rather than one passed by hand. This joy of the kingdom, proclaimed in the life, the words, and the ministry of Jesus, comes, Routley maintains, from the awareness of trajectory—the path of God's Word to us—and the awareness of conversation—the dialogue of love between God and humankind. Jesus fully reveals this pattern, this shape of God's Word to us, in order to teach us how God relates to us and how we are to relate to one another. He spoke God's truth and love not by encasing it is any system, moral or otherwise, but by "living it, acting it, and being it."[15] Our share in the joy of the kingdom is "the laughter, the pure pleasure of standing in the direct line of the trajectory of the Word of God."[16] Moreover, this joy is the result of the free conversation between God and us. Our response, our "Yes" to God's "Yes" to us in Christ, is just as important to this conversation because it respects our freedom and deepens the relationship of love between God and us.

The Scriptures are not, in Routley's understanding of them, a source book for passing on information or instruction about God or human life. That would deny the pattern of trajectory and conversation in them. They are the expression of God's offer of eternal life through the death and resurrection of Jesus, the Word Incarnate. Scripture provides, it is true, "proof" of this Word of God in our history, but along with this new meaning for our lives, it communicates the offer of joy, blessedness in the reality of this conversation between God and the human family. This joy that is essential in the Scriptures is like:

> *The human joy of taking the difficult catch. The human joy of anticipating the demand and finding one's anticipation correct. The human joy of conversation. The joy that accompanies every activity in which there is trajectory. That is what Scripture provides, and experience confirms it. The simple man. . .reads and finds comfort. The book speaks to him. . . . As he reads, something flashes up off the page at him, and he says, not the "yes" of the pupil or the "yes" of the slave, but a special kind of decisive "YES!" . . .The Bible is difficult enough to preoccupy the finest minds of any age; it is simple enough to comfort the death-bed of any half-lettered*

peasant. How can it be both these things, except it be the transcendent example of trajectory?[17]

These two images of conversation and trajectory in the scriptural Word of God are a key to Routley's understanding of how God communicates with humankind. They are also a mirror or reflection of our own communication in the Spirit. God's way of communicating with us as revealed in the Sacred Scripture—from its beginnings in the Old Covenant to its fulfillment in Jesus, the New Covenant—now, through the gift of the Spirit, becomes the pattern and shape of our communication with God and with one another. The images of conversation and trajectory are employed by Routley to explicate the reality of this communication of the life and joy of the Kingdom.

Routley speaks in his more recent writings of another quality that is related to the image of conversation: maturity.[18] Good, authentic conversation in human living reveals a maturity in persons, a growing up into our full human stature. Routley notes that Scripture can be read and understood as the story of how the human race struggles toward religious maturity:

> . . . *The Old Testament is a story about growing up, and about our resistance to growing up . . . . The New Testament is a confrontation with what it really means to hope for maturity . . . and that, having accepted the need to look for maturity, each of us must after all subject himself to a miracle in order to be put on the road to it—the miracle which includes repentance, conversion, sanctification, justification, and all the rest of the program right down to the beatific vision.*[19]

The joy and blessedness of the beatitudes belong, therefore, to those who are mature in Christ: the pure of heart, the gentle of spirit, the compassionate of soul, the patient and merciful, those who are self-forgetful. Such maturity brings a new kind of joy, that of the Kingdom of God.

This mark of maturity is linked closely with the images of conversation and trajectory in Routley's understanding of the scriptural Word of God as base and pattern of God's gift of his own life to the human family. They provide a framework and foundation for his understanding of how God's Word provides direction and principles for a theological understanding of music in Christian worship.

Public worship is a significant and essential activity of Christian believers, wherein the Word of God is proclaimed and preached to a specific congregation. Let us turn to Routley's use of the image of conversation and trajectory as operative and verified in the worship context.

2) *Free-Church Worship and the Images of Trajectory and Conversation*

Erik Routley is a representative of the free-church tradition, or the dissenting tradition, which includes, for example, the Congregational, Baptist, and Presbyterian denominations.[20] In the origins of this tradition, a complete freedom of worship was encouraged, that is, a worship of the Spirit that was not tied down to the printed word or to an ancient tradition. A prescribed formula of common prayer, or a set ritual form, was not necessary for public worship. Extempore prayer, the preaching of the Word of God as revealed in Scripture and directed by the Spirit, and the administration of the Gospel sacraments (Baptism and the Lord's Supper) were the touchstones of free-church worship.

An ideal free form of worship, Routley asserts:

> . . . *with nothing prescribed . . . implies that men are walking with God as friends, and can speak to Him without formality of ceremony. It implies that formality and ceremony are in the end born of fear. . . . A person whom you do not know very well must be treated with reserve. It is not so between close friends, and therefore it is not so between converted and covenanted Christian believers and their God.*[21]

This kind of worship would seem to verify unambiguously the pattern of trajectory and conversation, and to give evidence of a maturity in Christ of those worshiping. But it assumes that not only are the worshipers authentically free in the presence of their God, but that they are really free with one another. It assumes that their covenant with each other is complete, that they hold "all things in common" (Acts 2:44). The ideal free form of worship demands a great depth of freedom and commitment to God and with one another. History has shown that the dynamics and implications of the images of trajectory and conversation rooted in the revealed Word of God are not always carried through in the worship context.

A realistic free form of worship involves the tension of intimacy and ceremony;[22] or, another way of expressing it, the tension of freedom and pedagogy. In the history of actual free-church worship, people have chosen one pole or the other of the tension. But each pole has its inherent dangers: intimacy can lead to possessiveness, a crowding in on one's neighbor; ceremony can become empty formality; freedom can become irresponsibility and shallowness; pedagogy may result in mere instruction and information. Authentic worship in the free-church tradition should manifest at every level the dynamic of trajectory and conversation. As Routley states:

> It [worship] must reflect as faithfully as it can both the sovereign glory of God, the author of the Covenant, and the responsibility of man as its other party. It must neither exalt man unduly by drawing attention by its ingenuity and even beauty to his achievements and worthiness, nor depress him by subtly implying that he is not fit for freedom. It must reflect the fact that God's instructions come to men as they come in the teaching of Jesus, not as instructions in the teaching of Jesus, not as instructions come from the head of the firm to a junior executive. In short, it must, by evident submission to authority, be humble, and by evident respect of imagination and diversity, be hospitable.[23]

The experience of worship—communal prayer, the proclaiming and preaching of the Word of God, and the sacraments of Baptism and the Lord's Supper, when they are celebrated—should reflect the pattern and shape of conversation and trajectory as founded in the revealed Word of God.

There is always a creative tension and polarity in trajectory and conversation. This is no less true in the worship activity of believers. If the images of trajectory and conversation are operative in worship, as, for example, in the creative tension between intimacy and ceremony, freedom and pedagogy, a vitality and dynamism are maintained in the worship activity. And God is given room and space to break through to us, to reveal, to unveil God's self unexpectedly in the context of public worship in order to be united intimately and unreservedly to the worshipers. "This is the precious inheritance of free worship,"[24] Routley says. As an adherent of the free-church tradition, he clearly affirms the place of ceremony (a structure or order of service that may be prescribed) that permits trajectory, in order to guarantee that all those who worship together will have the freedom to be open to the gift of the "unveiled moment."[25] At the same time, he is concerned that the worship forms of the liturgical churches also allow and be receptive to the free gift of God's self to those worshiping.

The images of trajectory and conversation, for Routley, closely relate to the symbolic form of communication. This symbolic mode of communication imparts meaning on many levels. Because of the dynamics of trajectory and conversation operative in authentic public worship, there is a different way a group prays or one preaches in that context. Praying and preaching are symbolic acts. One does not pray or preach in a didactic or factual fashion, but symbolically. The symbolic mode of communication contains both the intellectual (or "reasonable,"[26] in Routley's phrase), and affective components. Symbolic communication does not deny either element, but it involves more than either one of them taken separately. In both the free-church tradition and the liturgically structured tradition, the symbolic structure or form of communication is found.

Prayer, in the liturgical churches, is symbolic because, through the use of familiar words, it stirs up and awakens the prayerful response of the worshipers. Prayer, when it is a symbolic act, touches and communicates to us more deeply than simple facts of information. Similarly, in the dissenting tradition, prayer is symbolic. As Routley affirms:

> . . . *The Dissenter's prayer, of whichever kind it be, is no less symbolic than the Catholic's prayer. If any Dissenting minister, speaking in his people's presence the words which he believes he is given to speak, believes that all his congregation is following every word he says, attending fully both to the words and to their collective sense, he lives in a dream. . . . To believe that is to believe that prayer is a kind of instruction. . . .*
>
> *Dissenting prayer, whether prepared or unprepared, is symbolic. . . . It should have precisely the purpose that liturgical prayer has—that of stirring up prayer in the worshiper.*[27]

The symbolic nature of prayer in public worship in any tradition affirms both the rational and emotional elements comprising it, but it also contains a deeper dimension of human communication. Every aspect of public worship shares in this symbolic structure or mode of communication. The free-church tradition of worship is not, for all its freedom, less symbolic in its forms of worship.

> *If Dissent wishes to defend its "freedom" of worship, it should defend it on the ground that there is room in it for "trajectory"—for imagination, for conversation; it should manifest in its practices what it believes to be the truth about communication.*[28]

Trajectory and conversation imply a symbolic level of communication. But, as in the prayer forms, other worship activities (such as preaching) operate and communicate symbolically as well.

Preaching the Word of God among a gathered congregation for worship is, in the free-church tradition, central to the worship. This act, like that of praying, is also symbolic. It is not instruction or information, issuing commands or giving facts. Preaching *contains* those elements but its deepest meaning is more than all that. In Routley's view, preaching is:

> . . . *the setting forth of the Gospel in words, the rational encounter with the mind of the congregation, the symbolic pro-*

clamation of the Good News as relevant to the immediate situation in which the Word is preached.[29]

A sermon, or the preached Word, forms an essential part of the symbolic structure of public worship. The principles of trajectory and conversation are verified in that activity of the worship service as much as they are found in prayer. For God's Word is communicated through the words of the preacher. These words of the preacher, directed by and penetrated with the power of the Spirit, are intended to touch and move the listeners at a deeper level of their lives. Merely uttering facts or giving instructions to a congregation does not constitute a sermon, or the preached Word, for such facts and instructions cannot communicate symbolically. They cannot move people to existential response and decision. They do not transform peoples' lives. The words of the preacher are an extension, as it were, of the Word of God proclaimed in the Scriptures. The sermon brings the Scriptures to bear on the present questions, struggles, hopes, and needs of this congregation. The sermon transposes the scriptural Word of God into an invitation to share God's life and love *today*. It calls the listeners beyond the point where they are at the present moment. It propels them into the future. The sermon can do this because it contains more than factual or instructional words. The preacher's words are a stimulus, a suggestion, a symbol that leaves a congregation free to welcome and encounter the living Word of God. The sermon should communicate more than can be grasped immediately by any one listener of the congregation or, in fact, by all the congregation. The preached Word communicates, then, in the symbolic mode. As Routley expresses it:

> *If my sermon, which comes from one voice, can be transformed by the Holy Spirit into a decision for every person present, different in every case, then I think each has heard the gospel "in his own language" and the pentecostal miracle has happened again. . . . If I do my work properly (i.e. preaching) and it is of the Lord, then through the words I say will come to that person a new conviction that God loves him, that life is worth living, that the devil has been conquered and can be conquered again.*[30]

The symbolic nature of preaching in public worship is preaching "with trajectory,"[31] in the image of conversation. These images of trajectory and conversation that Routley uses in his understanding of God's way of communicating to our world as revealed in Scripture, are reflected, or should be, in the word of preaching in free-church worship. If God has spoken to us in the mode of conversation and trajectory, the preached Word must do likewise. God's freedom and human freedom are thereby both affirmed. The Mystery of God and human dignity are thus both celebrated. God's Word and the human word of response meet in mutual respect.

Summary:

God's faithful love has been revealed to the human family first through the people of Israel and then through the humanity of God's own Word and Son. Through the outpouring of the Spirit, the church continues to proclaim this forgiving love of God in Christ. The Scriptures are the privileged expression of that revelation and communication of God to us. In the scriptural Word of God, Routley finds the shape, pattern, and purpose of the continual offer of God's self to us. He grounds his theology in this revealed Word. The images of trajectory, conversation, and, recently, maturity, bring out in more explicit fashion the pattern of divine-human communication in the Scriptures. As images, they express the principles, foundations, and direction for all Christian activity.

The public worship of the Christian community, and all that happens within that context, such as praying and preaching, is rooted in the pattern and shape of the revealed Word of God. Thus, the images of trajectory, conversation, and maturity operate and are verified in Christian worship. Hence, the worship of the gathered congregation mirrors and deepens the communication of the joy of the Kingdom of God for our lives.

Music is also an important dimension of worship. Its theological meaning will also be grounded in the pattern and shape of the revealed Word of God.

Chapter 4:
Church Music: A Ministry Toward Christian Maturity

The integrity of Christian worship demands that the "word"
that comes through the music shall be as charitable, but also
as alarming, as the word which comes through the Scriptures
which was spoken in the cross and resurrection of Christ.[1]

The Word of God, made flesh in the humanity of Jesus,
the Son of God, has been revealed in creation, in human history, and, finally, in the church. The trajectory of God's
movement toward us is communicated through the sacred
Scriptures. When these Scriptures are proclaimed and
preached among the gathered congregation, the Word of
God, through the Spirit, forms the worshipers into the People of God, into the Body of Christ, sent into the world to witness to the enduring love of God in Christ Jesus, In these
Scriptures, according to Routley, we have the ground of our
faith and can discover the pattern, the shape, and the principles for theological meaning and judgments in every area of
our Christian activity.

In the previous chapter, Routley's images of trajectory,
conversation, and maturity as operative in the scriptural
Word and in public worship were summarized. The question
of his theological understanding of music in worship can now
be taken up. Routley raises the same kind of questions that
Gelineau asks: How does music "speak" theologically in the
context of worship? What does music in worship "mean"
theologically? Or, as Routley says:

If somebody from the secular world comes and asks me what
we think we are doing when we play and sing in church, I
want to have an answer.[2]

Routley's theological basis for the meaning of music in
worship is not a musical judgment, i.e., whether a musical

work is good or bad as music, or even what style is more appropriate to worship—baroque, romantic, contemporary, etc. Nor can its theological dimension be located simply in its role as an enhancement or completion of the liturgical text or action, since, for Routley, Scripture grounds the theological meaning of music in worship. But most fundamentally, the theological point of music in worship is whether and how it conforms to the Gospel, to the death and resurrection of Jesus Christ. Does it express the newness of the Kingdom revealed in Jesus by his death and resurrection? Does it communicate to the worshipers the joy of the Kingdom revealed in Jesus by his death and resurrection? Does the music of worship lead the worshipers to a greater maturity in Christ? Does it spur the gathered congregation to a greater responsibility for the building of God's Kingdom in this world? These are questions that must be asked to determine whether the music in worship means something theologically. If church music frustrates the growth and encourages the immaturity of believers in their discipleship with the Lord, then it misses the theological point of its existence in worship. "This," says Routley, "is the heart of Christian criticism of church music."[3] The Scriptures reveal and communicate God's Word and Love as an invitation to become fully alive as human beings in God, to become free sons and daughters in the image of the Son, to attain the full stature of humanity in Christ. The music for worship, if it is to be theologically meaningful, must share, in its own way, the same purpose of God's communication to humankind as expressed in the Scriptures.

When the Word of God is proclaimed and preached within the gathered congregation, the worshipers are invited and challenged to respond to the conversation begun by God. In this proclamation and response, God forms and shapes and strengthens us so that we can be prophets and witnesses, communicating to the world the gift and challenge of the Good News in Jesus Christ. Jesus is the one who is the definitive form of the conversation in which God continually engages the human family. Jesus is the one who reveals the maturity to which all God's children are called, a maturity that includes both his cross and resurrection. This is the heart of the Gospel. And, Routley affirms:

> *Wherever you teach the Gospels, this is the emphasis that you are bound to find: discipline, leading to personal corporate happiness. Music is meant to adorn and express and enhance true Christian happiness. The Christian must pass through the regeneration of the Cross to achieve it. . . . Since he is in the service of that Savior, the keynote of his music will be victory; discipline will be necessary to that, but in the end subordinate to it. After the strife, the songs of Zion.*[4]

I will take up three areas of Routley's theology of worship music:

1) Music and the aesthetic in worship;
2) Scriptural background of music in worship;
3) Music and the Drama of Worship.

1) *Music and the Aesthetic in Worship*

In Routley's view, the art of music, like any art form, is an example of the image of trajectory at work. "Art," he says, "is a mode of human public conversation."[5] The artist is one who is attempting to engage another in a conversation, to evoke a free response to what he or she is communicating. The artist does not communicate by bare information or instruction but uses images (musical, choreographic, visual, etc.) that carry a wealth and depth of meaning to the recipient. An artist renounces the explicitness of meaning contained, for example, in a telephone directory, a price list, or a public notice. Art communicates the view, meaning, or value of reality of the artist. The particular art form contains more meaning than is explicit or that could be conveyed by mere statement of fact. In this sense, Routley believes that the artist always deals in trajectory. The poet, for example, is "throwing many balls at once, inviting the reader to catch as many as he can. Catching them is the human pleasure in contemplating art."[6] In "throwing the ball," the artist is initiating a conversation, inviting and expecting the joy of free response. Using a musical analogy, Routley likens the artist's communication of meaning to the way overtones are contained in, and accompany a fundamental tone or note in music. To hear the "overtones" in the artist's images is to receive the meaning being communicated. As he states:

> *In any art . . . there is a trajectory waiting for a response. . . . The artist . . . is not doing his work as an artist if he does not add interpretation to information, overtone to fundamental.*[7]

The art of music, according to Routley, exemplifies this trajectory pattern even more than the other arts. Poetry, for example, employs the medium of words to speak artistically. But words can also be a communication of information or instruction. Words, in this sense, are useful, not artistic. Music, for the most part however, communicates through sound and rhythm something more than what is merely useful, informational, or instructive. Beethoven's *Missa Solemnis* could hardly be called anything but art. The images of trajectory, conversation, and maturity make more sense here than the notions of information, instruction, or usefulness. Routley asserts that "Even most hymn tones are musically evocative enough to distract one's attention from the words to which they are set."[8] Nor can the artist explain his or her work with mere rational concepts. Otherwise, the art form would not be needed to communicate what the artist desires to communicate. Rather, the artist begins a conversation with another who might want to be a partner in this dialogue, to "catch the ball," so to speak.

Furthermore, it is the artist who uses the same method as Jesus used in speaking to the disciples, i.e., in parables. Routley expresses the importance of the artist in the communication of God's truth in this way:

> *Without a parable the artist never speaks. It is not that he wants to be obscure. It is that he so speaks that there is a risk of things becoming less intelligible if you do not "catch the ball," because if you do catch it you will have so much more than if he had passed it to you. What he says, in however*

private and personal a way he says it, he says more universally if he withdraws far enough to be able to throw it to you. He aims to communicate truth and also to give pleasure. This, the pleasure of trajectory, is the pleasure he is most concerned to give, and which to withhold would be to betray his being as an artist. If you crowd him, or ask him to crowd you, you will not hear what he says. He would rather, as it were, borrow Peter's boat and speak from the calmer isolation of the lake. What he says is clearer for the distance and the overtones; clearer because of all the relations with other things that are implied in its composite note.[9]

The artist, as Jesus does in his parables, invites us to go beyond the "letter," i.e., mere information, explicitness, usefulness, or instruction. Only the Spirit gives life. Artistic forms participate in some way in the life-giving Spirit.

Art, then, for Routley, is one of the manifestations of the Holy Spirit's action in the world. Everyone is an artist in some sense or other. Everyone is a self-revealer, a self-giver if he or she were permitted to be such. But it is especially in the worship of the gathered congregation that the aesthetic dimension can aid in the Spirit's work. To encourage and, in some places, restore the aesthetic in Christian worship does not mean simply more beautiful singing, more sophisticated music, or more performances of large cantatas. It means that the worshipers can "find that in the church's great public and corporate activity of demonstrating the faith, they can be—wholly, joyfully, astonishingly—themselves."[10]

The aesthetic in worship, moreover, involves the whole activity of worship and those engaged in it—the musician, the architect, the painter, the minister, the preacher, the worshiper. They are all in a conversation with each other. The aesthetic element reveals clearly the image of trajectory at work. The gathered congregation, the church, indicates the direction and source of the trajectory and conversation. Music, as one of the aesthetic elements in worship, should aim at being good music (i.e., whose quality conforms to the discipline of music) that will stir up in those who listen to it the gift of the Spirit, bringing them closer to the Kingdom.

Music is not part of the worship in order to be impressive or to win praise; instead, the effect of music on the worshipers should be a deeper experience of God

> . . . near and far, God withdrawn, God intimately present; God reigning, God pleading; God serenely and sweetly ordering all things, God suddenly irrupting; Christ saying: "I judge no man," Christ hurling the furniture down the temple steps; Christ baptized of John, Christ transcending John; the Holy Spirit as the dove, the Holy Spirit as the fire. [11]

The music of worship should communicate the same God revealed in Scripture—faithful but always beyond our grasp and our categories. The same pattern of trajectory and conversation in the Scriptures is operative in the aesthetic elements of worship. Music does this because it is a kind of trajectory. In the music of worship particularly, there must be room for trajectory, room "for contradictory propositions to collide, fight, play and dance." [12]

2) Scriptural Background of Music in Worship

"The Bible," Routley maintains, "says virtually nothing about church music. . . ." [13] So much of our church practice in music is thoroughly untheological and unprincipled . . . that it is time we revised our notions of its connection with the ground of our faith." [14] Both the Old Testament and New Testament contain few specific statements about the theological justification of music in worship. But Routley is convinced that the theological principles and meaning of church music can be discovered and inferred from the Scriptures, "the story of mankind's struggling toward religious maturity." [15] In this story of deepening maturity—through preparatory, incomplete stages to the definitive event of revelation of the Good News of Jesus' death and rising and the sending of the Spirit—Routley draws out his theology of church music.

From the primitive song of Miriam (Ex. 15:20ff) to the elaborate worship of the Second Temple (Ezra and Nehemiah), music is employed in the worship of Israel's God. Singing and making music to the Lord is the religious expression of the natural desire to sing: "It is a good thing to give thanks to the Lord, to sing praises to thy name, O Most High" (Ps. 92:1). Israel's music, as well as all else, was in the total context of the Old Testament faith: the revelation of God's will and the people's response or lack of response. The Old Testament stage of humanity's growth in religious maturity is a source for understanding the moral teaching of the religious use of music in worship.

Routley affirms that in the earlier writings of Israel's religious history two traditions of sacred music can be found: the prophetic and the levitical. Both traditions in the Old Testament are important in the unfolding of the theological meaning of music in worship.

In I Samuel 9 and 10, the account of Saul meeting the bank of prophets "coming down from the high place with harp, tambourine, flute, and lyre before them, prophesying," (I Sm. 10:5) illustrates that the early tradition of prophets is not yet that of "the great moralists, social critics, political advisers, and preachers."[16] They were musicians and dancers—"folk artists"[17]—who in their own strange way recalled to the people the power and presence of God. In this tradition, folk singing and dancing appear to be closely joined in Israel's worship. In the prophetic tradition:

> . . . sacred music is something ecstatic, inspired, topical, . . . has its roots in human life with all its tragedy and all its brilliance—in Saul the beautiful and Saul the insane, in David the serene young singer who could cast out Saul's devils . . . and in David the arrogant autocrat who shamed himself with Bethsheba . . .[18]

The levitical tradition of sacred music emerges later in Israel's history. The order of Levites was established to care for the matter of worship and the performance of music within the worship (Num. 18:21; II Chr. 5:12). The worship of the temple required an order, a discipline. Thus, the music tradition in this context manifests an

> . . . impersonal, legislative, liturgical music, . . . music full of joy and splendor, no doubt, but professional, tamed, sacred.

Its genius is not in common life but in the holiness, the separateness of worship.[19]

The presence and complementarity of these two traditions of worship music in Israel's history indicate that music for worship cannot be adequately understood except as a joining, a harmonization, a complementarity of the prophetic and levitical traditions. And Routley sees a related theological principle at work here. Human life, when lived authentically and creatively, is a balance between the ecstatic and the disciplined elements. The creation story itself is a paradigm of human creativity:

Creation is, viewed from one point of view, an explosion of inspiration; viewed from the other, it is the reduction of anarchy and chaos to order.[20]

An artist knows that inspiration and form (order) go hand-in-hand. The music of worship is no exception to this principle. The balancing of inspiration and order in worship music will always be necessary.

Another theological point concerning church music is inferred from the Old Testament text: concern and compassion for one's neighbor. The prophet Amos' denunciation of the music of solemn assemblies (Amos 5:21-24) contains an important theological meaning for the music at worship. There can occur the separation between giving glory and praise to God and showing justice and concern for one's neighbor. Music in worship can become an end, an obsession, rather than an expression of faith and fidelity to the God who demands recognition of his initiative and sovereignty, but also requires that people be shown justice and mercy. This is the prior concern of all who profess faith in the living God revealed in the Scriptures. Without this theological perspective, "our church music will be of the kind which both displays the degeneracy of our theological thinking and encourages others to imitate that degeneracy."[21] Church music is theologically sound when it is a way of loving God and humankind at the same time. The view of music for worship given in the Old Testament view has moral implications because it is not only directed to God but to the building up of the people of God. It can become mere show, or external display or self-gratification, if its theological meaning and purpose is not both God's glory, and justice and mercy toward others. Church music, says Routley,

> . . . *ought not to be an abomination, but it is made so by the repulsive incongruity between its beauty and religious zeal and the state of things in the city slums.*[22]

The finality of music for worship is the recognition of God's glory and sovereignty as well as the dignity of humankind manifested through justice and mercy.

The New Testament texts contain few references to church music. But there are principles, an underlying direction, that can be inferred from these writings concerning the theological meaning of music in worship. The New Testament writings center on the decisive event of God's final revelation in the life, death and resurrection of Jesus and the outpouring of the Spirit upon the world, manifested clearly in the church. Whereas the Old Testament is characterized by the principle of law, the New Testament is distinguishable by the principle of grace. The Old Testament is a tutor, a pedagogy of obedience to God's covenant revelation. It teaches its adherents how to walk rightly and blamelessly before God. The New Testament writings reveal the "new" law in Christ: blamelessness will not save one; only God's free gift of love and the human response of faith—utter confidence in that prior gift—can radically free and bring to full maturity the human family. Jesus, as the final self-revelation and self-communication of God, came not to abolish the law and the prophets, but to complete and fulfill them in his own person through the utter surrender of his own life to the one he called "Abba." Routley expresses the difference between the two stages of God's revelation:

> *The law, looked at from one point of view, says that blamelessness, if it can be achieved, is sufficient. Our Lord insists that blamelessness will not save,. . . the teaching of Christ, which distinguishes two worlds: that where the best one can*

achieve is the avoidance of error, and that where, avoiding er-
ror as a matter of course, one aims for an infinite extension of
positive good.[23]

The New Testament is characterized by newness because of
the principle of grace. It invites and enables believers to be,
think, live, and act on a totally different level. It involves the
whole of one's life. God is not a fault-finding judge but the
God of the Kingdom wherein joy in doing God's will is normal. This newness is revealed fully in Jesus' own pattern of
being before God and among human beings: he went about
doing good; he loved his own to the very end; he lay down his
life for others; he invited others to share in that same desire
and mission. In following his pattern of seeking the greatest
good for others, through self-forgetfulness and renunciation
and even at the cost of one's life, the Christian believer
witnesses to the freedom and maturity of being sons and
daughters with Christ before God.

Routley finds in the Gospel, then, two theological principles that are particularly relevant to the understanding of
music in worship:

On the one hand, we have the principle that it is not the
avoidance of error but the generation of good that we are to
look for. On the other hand, we have the principle that the
Christian's goal must be maturity in Christ. . . Where church
music inhibits the growth of the Christian society to maturity
it is to be censured.[24]

Returning to the dynamics of art, he sees in art a good
analogy of this kind of difference between law and grace. Art
does not simply avoid error or lack of proportion and integrity, but through inspiration manifests something new. It expresses "an extension of goodness."[25] The art of music in
worship ought, all the more, to illustrate and witness to the
meaning, value and direction of the Gospel. If it participates
in the newness of the Kingdom revealed in Jesus, it will bring
a goodness and a maturity to those worshiping. The music of
worship, therefore, does not communicate the meaning of
the Gospel if it relies on the element of "transfiguration or
thrill"[26] as its main purpose. Rather, it ought to help the wor-

shipers in their journey to God, through and beyond the beauty of this world. It should contribute to the maturity of those who participate in this music. It should help them become more intensely alive to God and the world. Authentic worship music deepens in the worshipers the joy and blessedness of the Kingdom where "duty and delight meet,. . .a condition where what God wills and what delights his creatures is the same."[27]

From two other New Testament texts, Ephesians 5:19 and Colossians 3:16, Routley draws out another theological dimension of music—especially song—in worship. It is a symbol of Christian fellowship. As he expresses it:

> . . . *we may conclude that the author of these messages saw the song of the gathered company of Christians as a symbol of the unity in brotherly love. . .*[28]

The context of these passages is a description and exhortation concerning Christian life and how it is different from that of unbelievers. When Christians gather for worship, everything should be done in the service of fellowship and communication. The experience of some congregations, however, is that music is a divisive factor. It generates disunity and breaks down communication between the members of the worshiping community. There are the musical and the unmusical worshipers. There are worshipers with conflicting musical tastes. But all are present to worship God and grow in the unity and love of Christ. The music of worship must seek to serve the good of the whole congregation, to express and deepen the kind of fellowship and unity characteristic of Christians. Both the unsophisticated and sophisticated musical members of the worshiping community have come together for a reason that is not mainly musical. The music, therefore, must be in the service of the Gospel mandate itself: love of God and one's neighbor. Public worship and all communication within this setting are rooted in that same theological principle of the Gospel. Speaking of the composer of music for worship, Routley makes his theological point:

He is required not merely to compose for the delectation or el-evation of an audience, or for the diversion, however culti-vated, of musicians. He is composing what will express what is in the worshipers, that they may sing not for musical effect but in order to achieve the communal discipline, that reali-zation of the Unity of the Body, which is the necessity, the fabric, and the monopoly of the Church.[29]

The music of worship, then, is theologically meaningful when it proclaims and leads the worshipers to the God re-vealed in Jesus Christ and to the building up of the unity of his Body. Both the Old and New Testament texts provide the-ological insight to guide the role and use of music in public worship. The images of trajectory, conversation, and maturi-ty in the scriptural Word of God are to be just as present and operative in the music we use for worship.

3) *Music and the Drama of Worship*

. . . the church's business at worship is to show the whole man to himself, and to call forth the gifts and the responses of the whole man. . . . This will be possible only if the church's wor-ship is seen to be essentially not merely experience, not merely instruction, not merely an appeal to the will, but a drama which includes all these things and fuses them into a living whole. My contention is that drama does include all these things, . . . that worship is the authentic kind of drama. . .[30]

The image of "drama" to characterize public worship combines the other images that Routley uses to describe God's communication to the human family, namely, trajec-tory, conversation, and maturity. Drama refers to a kind of symbolic communication. And in a worship service, the various elements—such as praying, preaching, and music-making—are intended to communicate meaning on a deeper level than mere fact or instruction. They communicate some-thing of the divine-human conversation that goes on in the drama of life but is especially highlighted in the drama of communal worship. In every service of worship, the "script" of this drama connects with the drama of the human journey and pilgrimage depicted in the Old and New Testaments. The proclamation and preaching of the Scriptures in worship is "dramatically, or symbolically, to juxtapose and bring into relevant relation the two dispensations 'B.C.' and 'A.D.'—of life to which Christ is about to speak and of life to which he has spoken."[31] The worship of the gathered congregation is drama in the context of faith. It mirrors the pattern of drama found in the Scriptures.

Routley claims that worship is essentially drama because it is corporate action, an action performed by people set aside to do it and which involves an active audience. It is not the same thing as entertainment or amusement. Drama, correctly understood. . .

> . . .means the only way in which a community can achieve a corporate response to the fundamental data of life. For Christians the fundamental datum is God. . . .[32]

To misconceive drama as a kind of entertainment for a passive audience is to miss what is essential in authentic drama: the community involvement in a total response to life's fundamental data. Christians come together in worship to do a work together in the presence of their God. This work together, this drama, is a response to God's initiating call and action.

In emphasizing this understanding of worship as drama, Routley admits that there are a variety of worship activities in the Anglican, Catholic, and Protestant traditions[33] that already contains much dramatic action, e.g., Evensong, Tenebrae, Lessons and Carols, the Eucharist. In each of these traditions, however, Routley sees the need to revive and restore this image of drama to the whole worship activity. In his own tradition, where Scripture and preaching are central in an ordinary service, he states that this kind of worship is no less drama for its lack of movement or visual symbols:

> A Protestant service is, from one to the next, a new creation. It is strictly existential. It is an occasion when the eternal gospel is made new not only in preaching but also in the

ordering of every word, including especially the choice of the congregational hymns. . . . A service is not gathered around a single thought that the preacher has invented. It is a progressive drama in which everything has its proper place, and which misplacements will destroy at a touch.[34]

The point of understanding worship as drama is that it involves the whole person and the whole community in a participatory action that includes the use of words, music, silence, movement, touch, color, space, smells, and taste in its total response to the data of faith. Drama, like symbol, communicates meaning at a much deeper level than do statements of fact. Drama communicates in the way of conversation and trajectory. The drama of worship speaks of wholeness and maturity.

Music, like praying and preaching, is an important part of this drama of worship. It is a non-verbal symbol that expresses and communicates the meaning of God's revelation as much as does any other element of the worship service. For Routley, the question is *how* it plays its part in the unfolding of the drama of worship. Music, in the context of this drama, must be part of the "script." It is not a hastily added element but serves the whole impact of the drama that the worshipers are involved in. Music is used as part of the corporate response in the worship drama and not as a "concert hall" musical work. The image of worship as drama governs the practical use of music for worship, whether this music be hymns, anthems, psalms, or instrumental pieces.

Hymns, for example, in the free-church liturgy, are an integral element to the proclamation and preaching of the Word in a service of worship. They surround the worshiper "with the church's teaching, converging on the particular point which is being emphasized on that particular occasion."[35] A sense of the "dramatic" development of the worship is essential in the choice of appropriate hymns. They must be chosen:

. . . with a sensitive ear to their allusions, ... a neighborly concern that they shall be practically singable, and a very

careful use of the hymns that people regard as "their own" and that make it possible for them really to bring part of themselves into the drama of worship.[36]

Likewise, anthems are "at their best. . .expositions of Scripture through music."[37] They are intended to be a topical comment on the worship, as a scriptural tie between the service and the common life of the people. The use and position of the anthem in a worship service "ought to be entirely adjustable, according to its own character and do its part in the drama relative to the other parts."[38] Whatever music is employed in the context of this drama must be carefully worked into the whole development of the drama. Public worship as drama needs the power of music for communicating its meaning. Music, in its turn, serves the drama of worship, not by drawing attention to itself, but as a reinforcement of the words or action of the drama.

The drama of worship, then, is the communal response to the fundamental object of Christian faith: God revealing and communicating life in the person of the Word made flesh through the power of their Holy Spirit. The symbol of music forms one element of that communal activity. It is most effective and communicative of theological meaning when it is part of the unfolding of that drama, that corporate response of faith. That drama is centered in the person of Jesus Christ, whose death and resurrection is the source of Christian worshipers' full stature and maturity in Christ Jesus:

It is, I trust, non pietist platitude to claim that our music and our music-making should aim at being conformable to a gospel which tells of a crucified and risen Redeemer, and which lays on us all the duty and the delight of losing our lives that we may save them.[39]

Conclusion

I offer a brief conclusion to this book. It would be brash of me to think or to say that in these foregoing pages I have exhausted the thought of these two men on this topic of the relationship of music to Christian worship and its theological assumptions and dimensions. Nor, for that matter, have I explored much other rich and provocative material in their writings. Both Gelineau and Routley have written prolifically. I can only hope that I have touched upon some of their basic and important theological views on this issue of music and worship. My "conversation" with them through their writings has stimulated and challenged my own thinking and work in Christian worship music.

Let me suggest a few reasons why the reflections of these two men can help all of us, musicians (and other artists as well), theologians, and worshipers alike in our continued growth in the understanding and praxis of music in the context of our communal worship.

1). It would not be an exaggeration to say that the past thirty years or so have been a turbulent as well as a creative and productive stage in the church's life. This is especially true in every aspect of worship and liturgical reform but more so in the musical forms and repertoire of our worship. At the heart of this phase has been the Second Vatican Council and the promulgation of the *Constitution on the Sacred Liturgy*. The experience and reflection on the worship life of the Christian communities prior to and following upon the Council has been a major part of the lives of each of these authors for these thirty years or so. They have not been mere observers or spectators to these eventful times and decisions in the church's life. Rather, they have been personally involved and have been active, leading participants (with others, to be sure) in the music and worship of their respective churches. Both Gelineau and Routley (until his recent death) are reflective people to be reckoned with in this area because of their passionate commitment to, and their serious and continued reflections on this issue.

2). Both of them are artist-musicians who have recognized the importance of artistic expressions as a symbolic form of communication in the worship action of believers. They know from experience the struggle to be both artist and theologian when it comes to understanding the worship event that must combine both. To choose art over theology in worship is to misunderstand both and to deny to the community the richness and depth of both; finally it would leave the worshiping assembly and their activity of worship bereft of both. Each of them affirms the need of keeping a creative tension between the two for the good of the worshiping assembly.

3). Each of these men brings a deep faith, love, hope, and intellectual search and honesty to this issue. They have continually raised new questions in seeking to make our worship celebrations signs of hope of the coming Kingdom of God. Gelineau can still challenge liturgists and musicians toward better liturgy in his latest book when he says: "Solemnities are vain, words are empty, music a waste of time, prayer useless and rites nothing but lies, if they are not transfigured by justice and mercy."[1] This is indeed a challenge to our liturgical assemblies of today with so much oppression and misery in the lives of countless children of God. And Routley, too, in his own inimitable style in his latest work, can call the hymns of the church "delightful and dangerous things. . .(that) can stunt the growth and frustrate the pilgrimage of Christian souls; but they can also nourish and fortify. . ."[2] This is no light responsibility for musicians and liturgists. Gelineau and Routley don't give us easy solutions to complex issues, but they do give us the right questions and some directions to move toward.

4). Any new development is in danger of having its faddish and superficial moments. The renewal of worship forms in our day needs solid and serious theological thinking by those responsible for worship. Both Gelineau and Routley have shown a depth and breadth of vision in their reflections on music and worship, as well as a warmth, humor, and passion for this area of church life. God knows we all need a good dose of all these elements.

5). Finally, it is difficult to imagine, in these times, any creative or fruitful theological reflection occurring that is closed to the ecumenical dialogue taking place in the whole Christian church; or, for that matter, the dialogue with non-christian traditions and with the world at large. It is, I believe, of utmost importance for Roman Catholics, for example, to be open to the experience of the worship and music of other traditions. In the area of congregational singing and hymnody, for example, we would not know of, or fully understand the possibilities, the successes, the struggles and the failures of this important element of worship without the experience and reflection of fellow Christians, except that people like Routley have searched it out and articulated it so well. And likewise, Reformed and other Protestant traditions need to be open to the Catholic liturgical tradition and its experience of music and worship if they are to be open to the potential and need of richer worship forms in their own traditions.[3] The church in all its different traditions has a heritage of worship music. Can any of us allow ourselves to be closed in, isolated by our own small part of a greater tradition that in our own time—as we head toward the 21st century—invites us to make *our* own contribution to the church's worship music tradition?

I would not, for a moment, contend that *only* Gelineau and Routley have spoken intelligently and responsibly on this important issue. Nor that they have spoken the *last* word on the subject. Far from it. But I do think they have faithfully and persistently invited us to think and act responsibly in the area of worship and liturgical music if we are to give glory to God and bring about God's Kingdom by our music—and in all our symbolic gestures—when we gather to worship.

I conclude with F. Pratt Green's hymn text. It expresses poetically what I think Gelineau and Routley say, and all of us may want to say and put into action in our use of music at worship.

> When, in our music, God is glorified,
> And adoration leaves no room for pride;
> It is as though the whole creation cried:
> ALLELUIA!

How oft, in making music, we have found
A new dimension in the world of sound,
As worship moved us to a more profound
ALLELUIA!

So has the Church, in liturgy and song,
In faith and love, through centuries of wrong,
Borne witness to the truth in every tongue:
ALLELUIA!

And did not Jesus sing a psalm that night
When utmost evil strove against the Light?
Then let us sing, for whom he won the fight:
ALLELUIA!

Let every instrument be tuned for praise!
Let all rejoice who have a voice to raise!
And may God give us faith to sing always:
ALLELUIA![4]

Notes

Introduction

1. See Johannes Quasten, *Music and Worship In Pagan and Christian Antiquity.* Washington, D.C.: The Pastoral Press. 1983; Eric Werner, *The Sacred Bridge:* The Interdependence of Liturgy and Music in Synagogue and Church During the First Millenium. New York: Columbia University Press. 1959.
2. A brief glance at the bibliography will be proof enough of their interest, concern, and competence in this area.
3. As a point of interest, both Gelineau and Routley were main speakers at the 1979 Convention of the National Association of Pastoral Musicians in Chicago.
4. Given at the Liturgical Consultation held at Boston College, June 1983.

PART I: JOSEPH GELINEAU

Chapter I

[1]Joseph Gelineau, *The Liturgy Today and Tomorrow.* New York: Paulist Press, 1978. trans. by Dinah Livingstone. p. 30.

[2]Ibid., p. 31.

[3]The Bishops of the United States also stated this theological principle very clearly in the document, *Music in Catholic Worship* (1972). "Music should assist the assembled believers to express and share the gift of faith that is within them and to nourish and strengthen their interior commitment of faith . . . The quality of joy and enthusiasm which music adds to community worship cannot be gained in any other way. It imparts a sense of unity to the congregation and sets the appropriate tone for a particular congregation" (p. 5).

[4]Gelineau, J. ed. *Dans vos assemblées:* sens et pratique de la célébration liturgique. Paris: Desclée & Cie., 1971. Tome I p. 22. (N.B. All translations of the French texts are my own unless otherwise indicated.)

[5]Ibid., p. 18.

[6]Ibid., p. 21.

[7]Ibid., pp. 28-29.

[8]Ibid., p. 28.

[9]Ibid., p. 40.

[10]Ibid., p. 41.

[11]Ibid., p. 41.

[12]Ibid., p. 42.

[13]Ibid., p. 43.

[14]Ibid., p. 44.

[15]Ibid., p. 45.

[16]Ibid., p. 45.

[17]Ibid., p. 46.

[18]Gelineau, *The Liturgy Today and Tomorrow,* p. 51.

[19]____ ed. *Dans vos assemblées*, Tome I, pp. 46-47.

[20]____ "Balancing Performance and Participation" in *Pastoral Music,* vol. 3, no. 5, June-July 1979, p. 22.

[21]____ ed., *Dans vos assemblées,* Tome I, p. 61. Although he often uses "sign" and "symbol" interchangeably, he is well aware of the distinction and nuances between them. See pp. 62-63 of this work.

[22]Ibid., pp. 63-64.

[23]____ *The Liturgy Today and Tomorrow,* p. 98.

[24]____ *Dans vos assemblées,* Tome I, pp. 68-69.

[25]Ibid., pp. 70-71.

[26]____ *The Liturgy Today and Tomorrow,* p. 96.

[27]____ *Dans vos assemblées,* Tome I, p. 73.

[28]Ibid., p. 74.

[29]____ *The Liturgy Today and Tomorrow,* p. 99. Cf. Tillich's understanding of symbolism: "Every symbol opens up a level of reality for which non-symbolic speaking is inadequate. Let us interpret this, or explain this, in terms of artistic symbols. The more we try to enter into the meaning of symbols, the more we become aware that it is a function of art to open up levels of reality; in poetry, in visual art, and in music, levels of reality are opened up which can be opened up in no other way. Now if this is the function of art, then certainly artistic creations have symbolic character. . .But in order to do this, something else must opened up. . .namely, levels of the soul, levels of our interior reality.. . ." Paul Tillich, *Theology of Culture,* ed. by Robert C. Kimball, New York: Oxford University Press, 1959. pp. 56-57.

[30]Ibid., p. 100.

[31]____ "Balancing Performance and Participation" in *Pastoral Music,* p. 22.

[32]____ *Dans vos assemblées,* Tome I, p. xiv.

[33]Ibid., p. 144.

[34]Ibid., p. 153.

[35]Ibid., Tome II, p. 393.

[36]Ibid., p. 395. Cf. Dom Gregory Dix' "four-action" shape of the Eucharist: the offertory, the prayer, the fraction and the communion, in *The Shape of the Liturgy.* London: Dacre Press, 1945, pp. 48-50.

[37]Ibid., p. 404.

Chapter 2

[1]Gelineau, "Music and Singing in the Liturgy" in *The Study of Liturgy,* ed. by Cheslyn Jones, Geoffrey Wainwright, Edward Yarnold, S.J. New York: Oxford University Press, 1978. p. 440.

[2]See ch.1, note 7.

[3]Music in the context of worship is, for Gelineau, primarily song, but also includes instrumental music as accompaniment to liturgical song and as used without words. See "Music and Singing in the Liturgy," ibid., pp. 443-444.

[4]_____ "Les Assemblées liturgique et leur expression musicale," *Eglise qui chante* 118-119, mai-juin 1972, p. 38.

[5]_____ *Demain la liturgie,* Essai sur l'évolution des assemblées chrétiennes. Paris: Les Editions du Cerf. 1979. pp. 114-115.

[6]_____ "Balancing Performance and Participation" op. cit. p. 24.

[7]See chapter 1, p. 27.

[8]See C. Winfred Douglas, *Church Music in History and Practice:* Studies in the Praise of God. New York: C. Scribner's Sons, 1937.

[9]_____ *Dans vos assemblées,* Tome I, p. 63.

[10]_____ *The Liturgy Today and Tomorrow,* p. 97.

[11]_____ "What No Ear Has Heard. . ." in *Music and Liturgy* vol.5, no. 3-4, 1979. p. 91.

[12]_____ *Voices and Instruments in Christian Worship,* trans. by Clifford Howell, S.J. London: Burns & Oates, 1964. pp. 31-32. See also his more recent article: "Liturgie Poetique. Poetique liturgique," *Maison-Dieu* 150: 7-21. 1982, in which he considers the liturgy as an art form and the relation of the poetic elements to the liturgy and the liturgical action to the poetic elements.

[13]Ibid., p. 15.

[14]_____ *The Liturgy Today and Tomorrow,* p. 88.

[15]_____ "Music and Singing in the Liturgy" in *The Study of Liturgy,* p. 441.

[16]____ Ibid., p. 442.

[17]____ *Voices and Instruments in Christian Worship,* p. 27. See also his footnote 7, p. 13 on the use of words "mystery" and "sacramentum" and "sacred sign."

[18]____ "What No Ear Has Heard. . ." p. 93.

[19]____ *Voices and Instruments in Christian Worship,* pp. 27-28.

[20]Ibid., p. 45.

[21]____ "What No Ear Has Heard. . ." p. 89.

[22]____ *The Liturgy Today and Tomorrow,* p. 107.

[23]____ "What No Ear Has Heard. . ." pp. 89-90. See also "Are New Forms of Liturgical Singing and Music Developing?" in *Prayer and Community,* ed. by H. Schmidt, Concilium Series. New York: Herder & Herder, 1970. pp. 37-46.

[24]____ "What No Ear Has Heard. . .," p. 90. See also "Tradition, Création, Culture" in *Concilium* 182. ed. Mary Collins & David Power. Paris: Editions Beauchesne. 1983, pp. 21-33.

[25]____ "Music and Singing in the Liturgy" in *The Study of Liturgy,* p. 444.

[26]____ *Voices and Instruments in Christian Worship,* p. 38.

[27]Ibid., p. 37.

[28]____ *The Liturgy Today and Tomorrow,* p. 90.

[29]____ *Demain la liturgie,* p. 113.

[30]____ *The Liturgy Today and Tomorrow,* p. 91.

[31]____ "Les assemblées liturgiques et leur expression musicale" in *Eglise qui chante* 118-119, mai-juin 1972, p. 38. I am attempting to clarify the central points in Gelineau's theology of liturgical music. In no way does he deny or depreciate the element of beauty and goodness of form for liturgical music. His writings and his own musical compositions are witnesses to his concern for artistic beauty in liturgical music.

[32]Ibid. p. 39.

[33]*Constitution on the Sacred Liturgy,* ch. 6, par. 112, in *Papal Legislation on Sacred Music* by Robert Hayburn, Collegeville, Minn.: The Liturgical Press, 1979) p. 383. This paragraph continues and describes the nature of liturgical music: ". . .is to be considered the more holy, the more closely connected it is with the liturgical action, whether making prayer more pleasing, promoting unity of minds, or conferring greater solemmnity upon the sacred rites. . . ."

[34]____ "What No Ear Has Heard. . ." p. 92.

[35]Sometimes this prayer is called the prayer of thanksgiving, the

prayer of consecration, the anaphora, or the Canon. The classical structure includes these elements: initial dialogue, prefatio (praise for creation), Sanctus acclamation, post-sanctus (praise for redemption), epiclesis (invocation of Holy Spirit on bread and wine), institution narrative, memorial acclamation and anamnesis-offering, second epiclesis (invocation of Holy Spirit on the gathered people), intercessions, final doxology, and Amen.

[36]I refer the reader to the 4th section of the first chapter where the parallel between the present eucharistic rite of the Christian liturgy (i.e., preparation of the bread and wine, the prayer of thanksgiving, the breaking of bread and the partaking of the bread and cup) and Jesus' actions at the Last Supper ("He took bread, gave thanks, broke the bread, gave it to the disciples. . .") is explained. In this section, I am only taking the "giving thanks" element. For concrete examples of these eucharistic prayers, one can refer to the new prayer texts in the Roman Catholic, Anglican/Episcopalian, Methodist traditions.

[37]____ "La Prière eucharistique" in *Eglise qui chante* 135-136, juillet-aout 1974, p. 23.

[38]A clarification: within the whole eucharistic prayer, there are different movements and moods of prayer—praise, thanksgiving, supplication and a concluding doxology of praise. All the movements are not necessarily to be sung, or musically expressed. Nor would each be done in the same way.

[39]____ "Exemples de Réalisation" in *Eglise qui chante* 135-136, juillet-aout 1974, p. 24.

[40]____ "L'Ouverture de l'Eucharistie" in *Eglise qui chante,* ibid., p. 18.

[41]____ "Exemples de Réalisation" in *Eglise qui chante,* ibid., p. 27. This is a free, not a poetic, translation of the original French hymn.
[42]Ibid., p. 28.

PART II

Chapter 3

[1]Erik Routley, *Words, Music and the Church.* Nashville: Abingdon Press, 1968. p. 181.

[2]____ *Music Leadership in the Church.* Nashville: Abingdon Press, 1967. In his discussion of the musician and the Bible in Section II of the book, he states his position clearly, to avoid any charge of fundamentalism: "I hold that any question of any impor-

tance that a man wishes to ask concerning the moral or spiritual life will be found to be answered in the Bible, but that it will not be answered necessarily by direct instruction. . . . It is communicated more by *example*. . ." pp. 52-53.

³____ *Into a Far Country*. London: Independent Press Ltd., 1962. p. 156.

⁴Routley explains the etymological roots of the word "parable." I quote: "Now the word *parable* contains a Greek root *(ballo)*, which means 'I throw.' The verb and preposition, which together make up the original of *parable*, mean quite literally 'throw alongside' or 'throw past.' *Para* means 'past' or 'alongside' and is used (among other uses) in verbs that imply missing a mark. And although the 'throw' sense in *ballo* even in classical Greek was weakened so that it hardly meant more than 'place,' nonetheless there are other words for 'place' to which compounds of *ballo* were always preferred when there was the least suggestion of throwing 'from a distance,' and of deliberation rather than accident or habit in the action described. . ." ibid., p. 23.

⁵The word "trajectory" is used in ballistics and dynamics to describe the path taken by a bullet fired from a gun or ball thrown from a hand.

⁶Ibid., p. 23. This particular word and image is not retained extensively in his later writings, but the force and meaning of it is. See his *Words, Music and the Church* in which he talks about the "the drama of worship," pp. 129ff.

⁷Ibid., p. 26.

⁸____ *Conversion*. Philadelphia: Fortress Press, 1978. p. 39

⁹It should be noted that Routley, in his book *Into a Far Country*, develops the image of trajectory and conversation as operative in the social and political life of the world, and in the authority and government of the church. For the purposes of this work, I restrict its connection to that of worship.

¹⁰____ *Into a Far Country,* p. 26.

¹¹Ibid., pp. 27-28.

¹²Ibid., *passim,* esp. pp. 28-38.

¹³Ibid., p. 34.

¹⁴Ibid., p. 37.

¹⁵Ibid., p. 34.

¹⁶Ibid., p. 38.

¹⁷Ibid., p. 155.

¹⁸see Routley, "Christian Hymnody and Christian Maturity" in

Worship 51, Nov. 1977, pp. 505-523. Also *Church Music and Christian Faith,* Carol Streams, Ill.: Agape, 1968. p. 20, and elsewhere.

[19]____ "Christian Hymnody and Christian Maturity," p. 507.

[20]I am aware that there is much variety and development going on in these denominations of the free church tradition concerning the understanding of public worship. But it is beyond the scope of this book to go into this area. I refer the reader to Stephen F. Winward, *The Reformation of Our Worship,* London: The Carey Kingsgate Press Ltd., 1964.

[21]____ *Into a Far Country,* p. 104.

[22]The word "ceremony" implies *some* order of service, though not necessarily fixed or prescribed.

[23]Ibid., p. 109.

[24]Ibid., p. 112.

[25]Ibid., p. 112.

[26]Ibid., p. 115-117.

[27]Ibid., p. 114.

[28]Ibid., p. 117.

[29]Ibid., p. 117-118.

[30]____ *Music Leadership in the Church,* p. 108.

[31]____ *Into a Far Country,* p. 123.

Chapter 4

[1]____ "Contemporary Catholic Hymnody in its Wider Setting: Smaller Hymnals," in *Worship* 47: May 1973, p. 271.

[2]____ *Words, Music and the Church,* Nashville: Abingdon Press, 1968. p. 8.

[3]____ *Church Music and the Christian Faith,* Carol Streams, Ill.: Agape, 1978. p. 76.

[4]____ *Music Leadership in the Church: A Conversation Chiefly with my American Friends,* Nashville: Abingdon Press, 1967, p. 98.

[5]____ *Into a Far Country,* p. 40.

[6]Ibid., p. 44.

[7]ibid., pp. 45-46.

[8]Ibid., p. 47.

[9]ibid., pp. 52-53. See also "An 'Honest to God' Controversy" in *The Hymn* 18: 1967, pp. 18-19.

[10]____ *Words, Music and the Church,* p. 217.

[11]____ *Into a Far Country,* p. 132.

[12]Ibid., p. 132.

[13]"Church music," as Routley uses the term, means liturgical or worship music. See his book, *Twentieth Century Church Music,* New York: Oxford University Press, 1964, p. 8.

[14]____ *Music Leadership in the Church,* p. 54.

[15]____ "Christian Hymnody and Christian Maturity," in *Worship* 51, Nov. 1977, p. 506.

[16]____ *Music Leadership in the Church,* pp. 55-56.

[17]Ibid., p. 56.

[18]Ibid., p. 58.

[19]Ibid., p. 58.

[20]ibid., p. 59.

[21]Ibid., pp. 61-62.

[22]____ *Church Music and Christian Faith,* p. 9.

[23]Ibid., p. 15.

[24]Ibid., p. 20.

[25]Ibid., p. 17

[26]Ibid., p. 85.

[27]Ibid., p. 87.

[28]____ *Music Leadership in the Church,* p. 89.

[29]____ *The Music of Christian Hymnody,* London: Independent Press Ltd., 1957, p. 171.

[30]____ *Words, Music and the Church,* p. 173-174.

[31]Ibid., p. 184.

[32]Ibid., p. 177. Routley notes some interesting similarities of his notion of "drama" with the Greek dramas of the 5th century B.C. as expressions of religion, and also with some techniques of contemporary drama, e.g. the apron stage, "theatre-in-the-round" and audience participation.

[33]There is not a common agreement on whether to distinguish "Anglican" and "Protestant." I have kept Routley's classification as he speaks of them in his book, *Words, Music and the Church.*

[34]Ibid., p. 156.

[35]____ *Hymns Today and Tomorrow,* Nashville: Abingdon Press, 1964. p. 125.

[36]____ *Words, Music and the Church,* p. 164. Cf. another text of Routley: "A hymn, then, is not really a good hymn until it has been well written, well chosen, and well sung" from *Hymns and Human Life,* London: John Murray, 1952, p. 299.

[37]Ibid., p. 192.
[38]Ibid., p. 194.
[39]_____ *Church Music and the Christian Faith,* p. 137.

Conclusion

[1]Gelineau, J., *The Liturgy Today and Tomorrow,* p. 123.
[2]Routley, E., *Christian Hymns Observed:* When in our music, God is Glorified, Princeton, N.J.: Prestige Publications, Inc. 1982. p. 1 and p. 107.
[3]See Doug Adams, *Meeting House to Camp Meeting:* Toward a History of American Free Church Worship from 1620-1835. Saratoga, CA: Modern Liturgy Resource Publications. 1981.
[4]F. Pratt Green, taken from the *Lutheran Book of Worship.* Prepared by churches participating in the Inter-Lutheran Commission on Worship. Minneapolis: Augsburg Publishing House. 1979.

Bibliography

(I have compiled an extensive list of the publications (books, articles and musical scores) of each author for further reference.)

PART I: JOSEPH GELINEAU

BOOKS

Gelineau, Joseph *Antiphona: Recherches sur les formes liturgiques de la psalmodie aux premiers siècles.* Paris: Editions Fleurus. 1968.

_____ *Chant et musique dans le culte chrétien:* Principes, lois et applications. Paris: Editions Fleurus. 1962.

_____ *Cinquante psaumes et quatre cantiques.* trad. Bible de Jérusalem. Paris: Centre de Pastorale Liturgique. 1954.

_____ *Dans vos assemblées:* Sens et pratique de la célébration liturgique. Avec la collaboration de C. Braga et al. Tome I & II. Trans. of Nelle Vestre Assemblee. Paris: Desclee. 1971.

_____ *Demain la liturgie:* Essai sur l'évolution des assemblées chrétiennes. Paris: Editions du Cerf. 1976.

_____ *Deux cent soixante-cinq antiennes extraites des cinquante-trois psaumes et quatre cantiques.* Paris: Editions du Cerf. 1956.

_____ *Festival Mass.* ICEL/ICET Trans. For Unison, or mixed choir, congregation and organ. London: Boosey and Hawkes. 1974.

_____ *The Gelineau Gradual:* Responsorial Psalms for the Lectionary for the Sundays and Principal Feasts of the Liturgical Year; Antiphons from the Hymnal Worship II; Psalms from the Grail-Gelineau Psalter. Chicago: GIA Publications. 1977.

_____ *The Grail/Gelineau Psalter:* 150 Psalms and 18 Canticles. Text: The Grail. Psalmody: J. Gelineau. Complied and edited by J. Robert Carroll. Chicago: GIA Publications. 1972.

_____ *Le Guide du psautier de la Bible de Jérusalem.* Notes sur le genre litteraire et la signification chrétienne de chaque psaume par D. Rimaud. Introd., notes techniques et index par. J. Gelineau. Paris: Editions du Cerf. 1962.

_____ *The Liturgy: Today and Tomorrow.* Trans. by Dinah Livingstone. New York: Paulist Press. 1978.

_____ *La Liturgie, source et sommet de la vie chrétienne.* Paris: Centre Alleluia 1965.

_____ *Le Livre de l'assemblée.* Chants et psaumes du missel. en coll. Paris: Editions du Cerf. 1965.

_____ *Le Livre de la chorale.* 80 psaumes d'entrée et de communion. 300 antiennes pour participation de l'assemblee. en coll. Paris: Editions du Cerf. 1967.

_____ *Lucernaire:* chants, lectures et prière pour sanctifier la fin du jour. Paris: Editions du Chalet. 1959.

_____ *Musique sacrée et langues modernes.* en coll. Paris: Editions Fleurus. 1964.

_____ *Psalmody in the Vernacular:* the theory and application of the Gelineau method of psalmody. Gregorian Institute of America. 1965.

_____ *The Psalms:* a new translation. Translated from the Hebrew, and arranged for singing to the psalmody of Joseph Gelineau. London: Collins. 1963.

_____ *Les Psaumes.* trad. par R. Tournay, o.p. avec la collaboration de J. Gelineau et al. Paris: Editions du Cerf. 1964.

_____ *Le Psautier de la Bible de Jérusalem.* Paris: Edtions du Cerf. 1961.

_____ *Le Psautier français:* Version nouvelle pour la priére, la lecture publique et le chant, une proposition oecuménique. Sous la direction de J. Gelineau. Paris: Editions du Cerf. 1973.

_____ *Refrains psalmiques.* Paris: Edtions du Cerf. 1963.

_____ *Rinnovamento liturgico e musica sacra.* Commento alla Istruzione 'Musicam Sacram.' Extrait des *Ephemerides liturgicae.* 81. 1967. Roma: Ed. liturgiche. 1967.

_____ *Soleil levant.* Recueil de 9 pièces. Paris: Editions du Levain. 1966.

_____ *Thirty Psalms and Two Canticles.* Trans. from the Hebrew and arranged for singing to the psalmody of J. Gelineau. London: The Grail. 1958.

_____ *Triduum Pascal.* en coll. Paris; Centre de Pastorale Liturgique. 1954.

_____ *Twenty Psalms and Three Canticles.* Accompaniment edition. Chicago: GIA Publications. 1967.

_____ *Twenty-Four Psalms and a Canticle.* Trans. from the Hebrew and arranged for singing to the psalmody of Joseph Gelineau. Toledo: Gregorian Institute of America. 1956.

_____ *Voices and Instruments in Christian Worship:* principles, laws, applications. Trans. by Clifford Howell, S. J. London: Burns & Oates. 1964.

ARTICLES

Gelineau, Joseph "L'aménagement de la cathédrale de Cuernavaca," *Maison-Dieu* 70:115-116. 1962.

_____ "The Animator," *Pastoral Music* 4: 18-22. 1979.

_____ "A propos des assemblées liturgiques de petits groupes," *Questions Liturgiques* 54: 169-179. 1973.

_____ "Are New Forms of Liturgical Singing and Music Developing?" Trans. by L. Sheppard. in *Prayer and Community* ed. by H. Schmidt. New York: Herder and Herder. 1970.

—————————— "Les approches doctrinales," in *Liturgie et Vie Spirituelle* by P. Grelot. Extrait de Dictionnaire de Spiritualité 6. Paris: Beauchesne. 1977.

—————————— "Les assemblées liturgiques et leur expression musicale," *Eglise qui Chante* 118-119: 35-39. 1972.

—————————— "Balancing Performance and Participation," *Pastoral Music* 3:22-24. 1979.

—————————— "Le cantique populaire en France," *Maison-Dieu* 7:115-125. 1946.

—————————— "Celebrating the Paschal Liberation," trans. by V. Green, in *Politics and Liturgy* ed. by H. Schmidt. New York: Herder and Herder. 1974.

—————————— "La célébration des heures communautaires en petit groupe, individuelle," *Maison-Dieu* 105:150-61. 1971.

—————————— "Célébration du matin pour les jeudi, vendredi et samedi saints," *Maison-Dieu* 49:155-61. 1957.

—————————— "Célébration et vie," *Maison-Dieu* 106: 7-43. 1971.

—————————— "La célébration liturgique du mariage," *Maison-Dieu* 50:130-152. 1957.

—————————— "La célébration liturgique en 1976," *Maison-Dieu* 128:26-44. 1976.

—————————— "Le chant des psaumes en pays de Missions," *Rythmes du Monde* 8:14-19. 1960.

—————————— "Le chant de procession," *Eglise qui Chante* 6-7:5-11. 1958.

—————————— "Le chant du peuple, sa necessité, sa beauté," *Maison-Dieu* 60:135-147. 1959.

—————————— "Le chant, élément essentiel de la célébration du culte," *Maison-Dieu* 20:42-63. 1949.

—————————— "Chant et musique dans le culte chrétien," *L'Union* 770:21-24. 1962.

—————————— "Le chant religieux populaire dans le monde," *Maison-Dieu* 74:184-199. 1964.

—————————— "Le chant sacré du peuple, III. La participation du peuple à l'action liturgique par des chants bien adaptés," *Eglise qui Chante* 3:7-10. 1958.

_____ "Les chants dans le nouvel 'Ordo Missae'," *Maison-Dieu* 100:104-116. 1969.

_____ "Les chants de procession," *Maison-Dieu* 43:74-93. 1955.

_____ "The Chants of the Baptismal Liturgy," trans. by John Rogers, in *Concilium* 22, ed. by J. Wagner. Glen Rock, N.J.: Paulist Press. 1967. pp. 69-87.

_____ "Les chants populaires durant la semaine sainte," *Maison-Dieu* 49:149-154. 1957.

_____ "The Choral Structure of the Mass." cond. from *Collectanea Mechliniensia* in *Theology Digest* 14:124-28. 1966.

_____ "Commentaire des anaphores nouvelles," in *Assemblées du Seigneur, 2e serie.* Paris: Editions du Cerf. 1969.

_____ "Commentaire de la Constitution conciliaire sur la liturgie: La musique sacrée," *Maison-Dieu* 77:193-210. 1964.

_____ "Comment faire une célébration de carême?" *Union* 80:19-28. no. 694. 1954.

_____ "Concrete Forms of Common Prayer," *Studia Liturgica* 10:137-150, no. 3-4. 1974.

_____ "Le IIIe Congrès international de musique sacrée, Paris, 1er- 8 juillet 1957," *Maison-Dieu* 51:146-165. 1957.

_____ "Le Congrès international de pastorale liturgique, Assise," *Musique et Liturgie* 54:86-88. 1956.

_____ "La création de chants liturgiques dans les milieux monastiques depuis le Concile. Réflexions et questions à partir d'expérience françaises," *Maison-Dieu* 145: 49-65. 1981.

_____ "Le Culte en esprit dans un peuple en fête," *Maison-Dieu* 79:63-80. 1964.

_____ "La date de la dernière Cène," *Maison-Dieu* 43:165-67. 1955.

_____ "Dum supplicat et psallit Ecclesia: Renouveau du chant et tradition. Le Rôle des chorales." *Concilium* 2: 1965. pp. 57-62. Paris: Editions Beauchesne. 1965

_____ "Eglises-Assemblées-Dimanche. Réflexions et perspectives pastorales," *Maison-Dieu* 124:85-109. 1975.

_____ "L'Eglise, lieu de la célébration," *Maison-Dieu* 63:41-52.1960.

_____ "Les éléments de l'office et leur célébration." in *Célébrer l'office divin.* Paris: Edition Fleurus. 1967.

_____ "Enquête sur le chant religieux," *Maison-Dieu* 13:93-103. 1948.

_____ "Enterrements de l'après-midi et veillées mortuaires," *Maison-Dieu* 44:83-102. 1955.

_____ "The Eucharistic Prayer," *Music and Liturgy* 6: 6-10. 1980.

_____ "Les exigences du chant dans les traductions liturgiques. Problèmes actuels," *Maison-Dieu* 86:161-69. 1966.

_____ "Faut-il changer chaque année la veillée de Noël?" *Notes Pastorales Liturgiques* 35:11-15. 1961

_____ "Faut-il chanter les lectures?" *Musica Sacra* 65: 171-78. 1964.

_____ "Fonction et signification des principaux chants de la liturgie," *Eglise qui Chante 17-26* (9 articles). 1959-61.

_____ "Les formes concrètes de la prière commune," *Maison-Dieu* 116:7-18. 1973.

_____ "Les formes de la psalmodie chrétienne," *Maison-Dieu* 33: 134-172. 1953.

_____ "L'homélie, forme plenière de la prédication," *Maison-Dieu* 82:29-42. 1965.

_____ "L'hymne dans une liturgie rénovée," *Maison-Dieu* 92:43-59.

_____ "L'Institut de musique liturgique de Paris," *Maison-Dieu* 98:163-64. 1969.

_____ "Une Instruction de la S. Congregation des Rites sur la musique sacrée et la liturgie," *Eglise qui chante* 10:4-9. 1958.

_____ "Les interventions de l'assemblée dans le Canon de la Messe," *Maison-Dieu* 87:141-49. 1966.

_____ "Langue sacrée, langue profane," *Maison-Dieu* 53:110-129. 1958.

_____ "Les lieux de l'assemblée célébrante," *Maison-Dieu* 88:64-82. 1966.

_____ "Le lieu de la célébration: les données historiques et actuelles," *Art Sacre:* 1-2:1-32. 1960.

_____ "La litanie du Pape Gelase. Son intérêt historique et pratique," *Musique et Liturgie* 37:11-12. 1954.

_____ "Liturgie poètique. Poètique liturgique," *Maison-Dieu* 150:7-21. 1982.

_____ "Lo que llamamos 'el Ordinario.' Los 5 cantos del Ordinario: situacion, historia y significado biblico, funcion y forma, actores, catequesis infantil," *Phase* 5:326-384. 1965.

_____ "Marie dans la prière chrétienne des psaumes," *Maison-Dieu* 38:30-55. 1954.

_____ "Les mélodies des psaumes," *Maison-Dieu* 33:198-206. 1953.

_____ "Modalité et psalmodie," in *Célébrer l'office divin*. Paris: Editions Fleurus. 1967.

_____ "Le mouvement interne de la prière eucharistique," *Maison-Dieu* 94:114-124. 1968.

_____ "Music and Singing in the Liturgy." in *The Study of Liturgy* ed. by C. Jones et al. New York: Oxford University Press. 1978. pp. 440-454.

_____ "The Nature and Role of Signs in the Economy of the Covenant." reprint and trans. from *Catechèse: Revue Pastorale Catéchètique* 1964, in *Worship* 39:530-50. 1965.

_____ "La nef et son organisation," *Maison-Dieu* 63:69-85. 1960.

_____ "Notes à propos de l'encyclique sur la musique sacrée," *Musique et Liturgie* 50-51:36-42. 1956.

_____ "Notes sur le chant religieux populaire en français," *Maison-Dieu* 11:209-224. 1947.

_____ "Nouveau dossier sur chant et Eucharistie," *Eglise qui chante* 135-6: 12-18. 1974.

_____ "Nouveaux textes de chants pour la Messe," *Maison-Dieu* 96: 32-56. 1968.

_____ "Ordinarium Missae. Presentazione che cos' e l'Ordinarium Missae. Il Sanctus. Agnus Dei," coll. work. *Il Canto dell'Assembea* 4:1-33. 1965.

_____ "Pour un renouveau du chant liturgique en pays de Mission," *Revue Clergé Africain* 19:442-60. 1964.

_____ "Pourquoi tutoyer Dieu dans les traductions bibliques?" *Maison-Dieu* 62:30-31. 1960.

_____ "La prière des laïcs et le bréviare," *Christus* 8:533-552. 1961.

_____ "Psalmodier en français. Méthode complète de psalmodie," *Eglise qui Chante* 98. Doc. no.2. 1971.

_____ "Les psaumes à l'époque patristique," *Maison-Dieu* 135:99-116. 1978.

_____ "Quelques remarques en marge de l'Instruction sur la traduction des textes liturgiques," *Maison-Dieu* 98:156-162. 1969.

_____ "Réflexions sur l'histoire du chant des assemblées chrétiennes," *Musique et Liturgie* 65:67-69. 1958; 66:88-91. 1958.

_____ "Réforme liturgique, renouveau de l'Eglise," *Etudes* 320: 8-26. 1964.

_____ "Règles pratiques d'interprétation de la psalmodie en français," *Maison-Dieu* 33: 208-13. 1953.

_____ "La rénovation du chant liturgiques," in *La Sacra Liturgia Renovata del Concilio.* Studi e commenti intorno alla Constituzione Liturgica del Concilio Ecumenico Vaticano II. by B. Barauna, O.F.M. Torino: Elle di Ci. 1964.

_____ "Renouveau dans les lieux, les livres et les acteurs de la célébration," *Maison-Dieu* 84:23-37. 1965.

_____ "The Role of Sacred Music." trans. by Theodore L. Weston. in *Concilium* 2, ed. J. Wagner. Glen Rock, N.J.: Paulist Press. 1964.

_____ "Les rôles dans l'assemblée qui chante. I. Le rôle du célébrant. II. Le rôle du peuple chrétien." *Eglise qui chante* 9:5-9. 1958; 10:10-13. 1958. 11:3-8. 1959.

_____ "Rythme et psalmodie française," *Maison-Dieu* 33:173-197. 1953.

_____ "Les rythmes de la prière du chrétien," *Maison-Dieu* 73:71-94. 1963.

_____ "Le sanctuaire et sa complexité," *Maison-Dieu* 63:53-68. 1960.

_____ "Singing by the People," *Theology Digest* 9:155-59. 1961.

_____ "Situation et variété du cantique," *Eglise qui chante* 68: 2-10. 1966.

_____ "Structure chorale de la Messe et problèmes de musique sacrée," *Collectanea Mechliniensia* 48:573-597. 1963.

_____ "Le style de la langue liturgique," *Maison-Dieu* 86:141-151. 1966.

_____ "The Symbols of Christian Initiation." (Oral Presentation, trans. and rewritten and ed. by T. Guzie) in *Becoming a Catholic Christian*. ed. by W. Reedy. New York: Sadlier Press. 1979. pp. 190-196.

_____ "Une technique à retrouver: le bon usuage d'un modèle dans les prières liturgiques," *Maison-Dieu* 114: 85-96. 1973.

_____ "Tradition-Création-Culture." *Concilium* 182. ed. M. Collins & D. Power. Paris: Editions Beauchesne. 1983. pp. 21-33.

_____ "Traduire, transposer, récréer les textes liturgiques en français," *Maison-Dieu* 81:75-89. 1965.

_____ "Vingt-quatre psaumes et le Magnificat," *Maison-Dieu* 33:93-94. 1953.

_____ "What No Ear Has Heard," *Music and Liturgy* 5:86-93. 1979.

_____ "Where is our Liturgy Going?" *Today's Parish* 12:18-22. 1980.

PART II: ERIK ROUTLEY
BOOKS

Routley, Erik.   *Ascent to the Cross.* New York: Abingdon, 1962.

             Beginning the Old Testament. Studies in Genesis and Exodus for the General Reader. Philadelphia: Muhlenberg Press. 1962.

             Christian Hymns. with K. Parry. London: Student Christian Movement Press. 1956.

             Christian Hymns: An Introduction to their Story. Cassette. Princeton, N.J.: Prestige Publications. 1980.

             Christian Hymns Observed: When in our Music God is Glorified. Princeton, N.J. Prestige Publications. 1982.

             The Church and Music: An Enquiry into the history, the nature and the scope of Christian Judgment on Music. London: Duckworth. 1950.

             Church Music and the Christian Faith. Carol Stream, Ill.: Agape. 1978.

             Church Music and Theology. London: SCM Press Ltd. 1959.

             Come Redeemer: For Mixed Voices SATB with organ. Chapel Hill, N.C.: Hinshaw Music, Inc. 1976.

             Companion to Congregational Praise ed. by K. Parry with notes on the music by Eric Routley. London: Independent Press. 1953.

             Companion to Festival Praise: a Hymn Service. Chapel Hill, N.C.: Hinshaw Music, Inc. 1979.

             Companion to Westminster Praise. Chapel Hill, N.C.: Hinshaw Music, Inc. 1977.

             Congregationalists and Unity. London: Mawbray. 1962.

             Conversion. Philadelphia: Fortress Press 1960.

             Creeds and Confessions: the Reformation and its Modern Implications. London: Duckworth. 1962.

             Ecumenical Hymnody. London: Independent Press. 1959.

_____ *Ecumenical Praise*. ed. board. Carol Stream, Ill.: Agape. 1977.

_____ *The English Carol*. Westport, Conn.: Greenwood Press. Reprint 1973.

_____ *English Religious Dissent*. Cambridge: University Press. 1960.

_____ *An English-Speaking Hymnal*. Collegeville, Minn.: The Liturgical Press. 1979.

_____ *Exploring the Psalms*. Philadelphia: Westminster Press. 1975.

_____ *Festival Praise:* A Hymn Service. Compiled by E. Routley. Chapel Hill, N.C.: Hinshaw Music, Inc. 1979.

_____ *25 Festive Hymns for Organ and Choir*. Minneapolis, Minn.: Augsburg Press. 1982.

_____ *The Gift of Conversion*. Philadelphia: Mulenberg Press. 1955.

_____ *The Hymns and Ballads of Fred Pratt Green*. Foreword. Carol Stream, Ill.: Hinshaw Music, Inc. 1982.

_____ *Hymns Ancient and Modern For Use in the Services of the Church, with accompanying Tunes*. London: W. Clowes. 1909.

_____ *Hymns and Human Life*. London: John Murray. 1959

_____ *Hymns and the Faith*. Greenwich, Conn.: Seabury Press. 1956.

_____ *Hymns for Celebration:* A Supplement for use at Holy Communion today. Croydon, Eng.: Royal School of Church Music. 1974.

_____ *Hymns Today and Tomorrow*. Nashville: Abingdon Press. 1964.

_____ *Hymn Tunes: An Historical Outline*. Croydon, Eng.: Royal School of Church Music. 1964.

_____ *I'll Praise My Maker*. A Study of the hymns of certain authors who stood in or near the tradition of English Calvinism, 1700-1850. London: Independent Press. 1951.

_____ *Into a Far Country:* Reflections upon the Trajectory of Divine Word, and upon the Communication in Affairs Human and Divine of the

Imperative and the Indicative. London: Independent Press. Ltd. 1962.

——————— *Is Jazz Music Christian?* London: Epworth. 1964.

——————— *Issac Watts: 1674-1748.* London: Independent Press. 1961.

——————— *The Man For Others.* An important contribution to the discussions inspired by the book 'Honest to God'. New York: Oxford University Press. 1964.

——————— *Martin Shaw: A Centenary Appreciation.* London: E.M. Campbell. 1975.

——————— *Music Leadership in the Church:* A Conversation Chiefly with my American Friends. Nashville: Abingdon Press. 1967.

——————— *The Music of Christian Hymnody:* A Study of Hymn Tunes since the Reformation, with Special Reference to English Protestantism. London: Independent Press. 1964.

——————— *The Music of Christian Hymns.* Chicago: GIA. Publications. 1981.

——————— *Music, Sacred and Profane:* Occasional Writings on Music, 1950-58. London: Independent Press. 1960.

——————— *The Musical Wesleys:* A historical survey of important contributions made by the Wesleys to church music in the 18th and 19th centuries. Musical excerpts throughout. New York: Oxford University Press. 1968.

——————— *New Songs for the Church.* Norfolk, Eng.: Galliard. 1969.

——————— *The Organist's Guide to Congregational Praise.* London: Independent Press. 1957.

——————— *A Panorama of Christian Hymnody.* Collegeville, Minn.: Liturgical Press. 1979.

——————— *The Prayer of Manasseh.* Chapel Hill, N.C.: Hinshaw Music, Inc. 1977.

——————— *The Puritan Pleasures of the Detective Story:* A Personal Monograph. London: Gollancz. 1972.

——————— *O Ruler of the Universe.* Chapel Hill, N.C.: Hinshaw Music, Inc. 1977.

_____ *Saul Among the Prophets.* abridged ed. Nashville, Tenn.: The Upper Room. 1972.

_____ *Saul Among the Prophets and other Sermons.* London: Epworth Press. 1971.

_____ *A Short History of English Church Music.* London: Mowbray, 1977.

_____ *Sing We Triumphant Hymns of Praise.* SATB with organ and brass. Chapel Hill, N.C.: Hinshaw Music, Inc. 1978.

_____ *Songs of Thanks and Praise.* ed. Chapel Hill, N.C.: Hinshaw Music Inc. 1980.

_____ *The Story of Congregationalism Briefly Told.* London: Independent Press. 1961.

_____ *The Study of Congregationalism.* London: Independent Press. 1961.

_____ *Thomas Goodwin.* London: Independent Press. 1961.

_____ *Twentieth Century Church Music.* New York: Oxford University Press. 1964.

_____ *Two For Pentecost.* SATB with organ. Chapel Hill, N.C.: Hinshaw Music, Inc. 1978.

_____ *University Carol Book:* A Collection of Carols from Many Lands, for All Seasons. ed. London: Freeman. 1961.

_____ *Westminster Praise.* ed. and arranged. Chapel Hill, N.C.: Hinshaw Music, Inc. 1976.

_____ *The Wisdom of the Fathers.* Naperville: SCM Book Club. 1957.

_____ *Words of Hymns: A Short History.* Croydon, Eng.: Royal School of Church Music. 1963.

_____ *Words, Music and the Church.* Nashville: Abingdon Press. 1968.

ARTICLES

Routley, Erik. "Agreed Statement: A Protestant View," *Expository Times* 83: 360-3. 1972.

_____ "Amen and Christian Hymnody," *Reformed Liturgy and Music:* Winter 1979, 19-23.

_____ "The Background of the English Renaissance in Hymnody," *The Hymn* 28:64-66. 1977.

_____ "British Look at the Worship Book," *Theology Today* 31: 214-20. 1974.

_____ "Cantate Domino (4th ed.)," *Reformed World* 32: 315-22. 1973.

_____ "Can We Enjoy Hymns?" *Music Ministry* April 1977:28-29.

_____ "Charles Wesley and Matthew Henry," *Congregational Quartely* 33:345-51. 1955.

_____ "Christian Hymnody and Christian Maturity," *Worship* 51: 505-23. 1977.

_____ "The Chorale Book for England, 1863," *Bulletin* for the Hymn Society of Great Britain and Ireland 5: 173-186. 1963.

_____ "Church Music: the Dilemma of Excellence," *Pastoral Music* 3:29-33. 1979.

_____ "Church Music and Hymnody: Browsing among Recent Books," *Worship* 53: 404-13. 1979.

_____ "Church Musician and His Faith," *Religion in Life* 32:287-93. 1963.

_____ "Church's Authority in a Vulgar Age," *London Quarterly and Holborn Review* 183:59-63. 1958.

_____ "Consular Horse," *Christian Century* 78: 343. 1961.

_____ "Contemporary Catholic Hymnody: an Afterword," *Worship* 47:417-23. 1973.

_____ "Contemporary Catholic Hymnody in its Wider Setting," Pt. I: The Larger Hymnals. *Worship* 47:194-211. Apr. 1973. Pt. II: The Smaller Hymnals. *Worship* 47:258-73. May 1973. Pt. III: Foreign Books and Liturgical Worship. *Worship* 47:322-37. June-July 1973.

_____ "Critic's Corner: Musicians and Ministers," (Reply to W.H. Scheid) *Theology Today* 20:274-6. 1963.

_____ "The Eucharistic Hymns of Isaac Watts," *Worship* 48:526-35. 1974.

_____ "Evangelism and Modern Man," *Christian Century* 76: 799-801. 1959.

_____ "Expediency or the Will of God," *London Quarterly and Holborn Review* 187:197-201. 1962.

_____ "The Gender of God: A Contribution to the Conversation." Reply to G.R. Schmidt. *Worship* 56:231-39. 1982.

_____ "A Hole in the Heavens," (Preaching on the Feast of St. Stephen) *Theology Today* 34:294-298. 1977.

_____ "An 'Honest to God' Controversy," *Bulletin* of the Hymn Society of Great Britain and Ireland 6:66-71. 1966.

_____ "A Hymn Competition of 95 Years Ago," *The Hymn* 7: 105-110. 1956.

_____ "Hymnody 1981-82: a Quiet Year," *Worship* 56:503-12. 1982.

_____ "Hymnody: our Annual Roundup," *Worship* 54:446-55. 1980.

_____ "Hymnody and related matters: our Annual report," *Worship* 55:518-28. 1981.

_____ "Hymns A & M: Four Supplements, 1889-1980," *English Church Music* ed. by P. Phillips. Croydon, Eng.: Royal School of Church Music. 1980. pp. 36-49.

_____ "Hymns and Music in Church Music," *Union Seminary Quarterly* 18:235-42. 1963.

_____ "Hymns Probable and Improbable." in *English Church Music:* A Collection of Essays. 1966. Croydon, Eng.: Royal School of Church Music. 1966. pp. 16-29.

_____ "Hymns: a Roundup for 1977," *Worship* 52:108-20. 1978.

_____ "Hymns: Stop the Plane, I want to Get Off," in *English Church Music:* A Collection of Essays. Croydon, Eng.: Royal School of Church Music. 1974. pp. 10-17.

_____ "Hymn Writers of the New English Renaissance," *The Hymn* 28:6-10. 1977.

_____ "An Interview with Erik Routley," by H. Eskew. *The Hymn* 32:198-206. 1981.

_____ "Music and Churchmanship," *Congregational Quarterly* 28:31-40, 1950.

_____ "Musicians and Ministers," *Theology Today* 20:274-6. 1963.

_____ "A National Hymnal?" *Worship* 49:263-71. 1975.

————————— "A New Book of Worship for a New Church," *Worship* 48:413-20. 1974.

————————— "The New Lutheran Book of Worship: A Preview of the Hymns," *Worship* 52:403-408. 1978.

————————— "The Notion of Sacred Music," in *Christianity in its Social Context* ed. by Gerard Irvine. London: S.P.C.K. 1962, pp. 54-71.

————————— "On The Billy Graham Song Book," *The Hymn* 6:26,36. 1955.

————————— "On the Display of Hymn Texts," *The Hymn* 30:16-20. 1979.

————————— "On Growing Quietly," *Christian Century* 78:727. 1961.

————————— "Percy Dearmer, 20th Century Hymnologist," *The Hymn* 19:74-80. 1968.

————————— "Prayers We Have in Common: The Musical Implications," *Worship* 47:137-43. 1973.

————————— "A Private Hymn Book from Scottish Congregationalism," *Bulletin* of the Hymn Society of Great Britain and Ireland 4:58-61. 1961.

————————— "Progress Report in Hymnody," *Worship* 49:393-9. 1975.

————————— "The Psalms in Today's Church," *Reformed Liturgy and Music,* November 1980. pp. 20-26.

————————— "Reflections on Reading the Essential Question," *Worship* 54:169-79. 1980.

————————— "Sexist Language: A View from a Distance," *Worship* 53:2-11. 1979. Also in *The Hymn* 31:26-32. 1980.

————————— "Singing about the Cross," *Liturgy* 1:64-68. 1980.

————————— "Six Great Moments in Twentieth Century Hymn Music," *Church Music Quarterly* April 4. 1979.

————————— "Spiritual Resonances in Hymnody," *Reformed Liturgy and Music,* vol. 16, no. 3.pp. 120-125.

————————— "Text for a Religious Aesthetic," *Theology Today* 17:192-9. 1960.

————————— "Theology and Practice of the Sect," *London Quarterly and Holborn Review* 188:99-104. 1963.

————————— "Things are Looking Better," *Worship* 50:43-9. 1976.

_____ "A Vigorous Year in Hymnology," *Worship* 51:120-26. 1977.

_____ "Vocabulary of Church Music," *Union Seminary Quarterly Review* 18:135-47. 1963.

_____ "What Remains for the Modern Hymn Writer to Do?" *Congregational Quarterly* 32:322-27. 1954.

_____ "Worship Song 1905," *Bulletin* of the Hymn Society of Great Britain and Ireland 5:225-234. 1964.

_____ "Worship: Talking with God, Ourselves, Others," *Thesis Theological Cassettes* 11: no. 7. 1980.